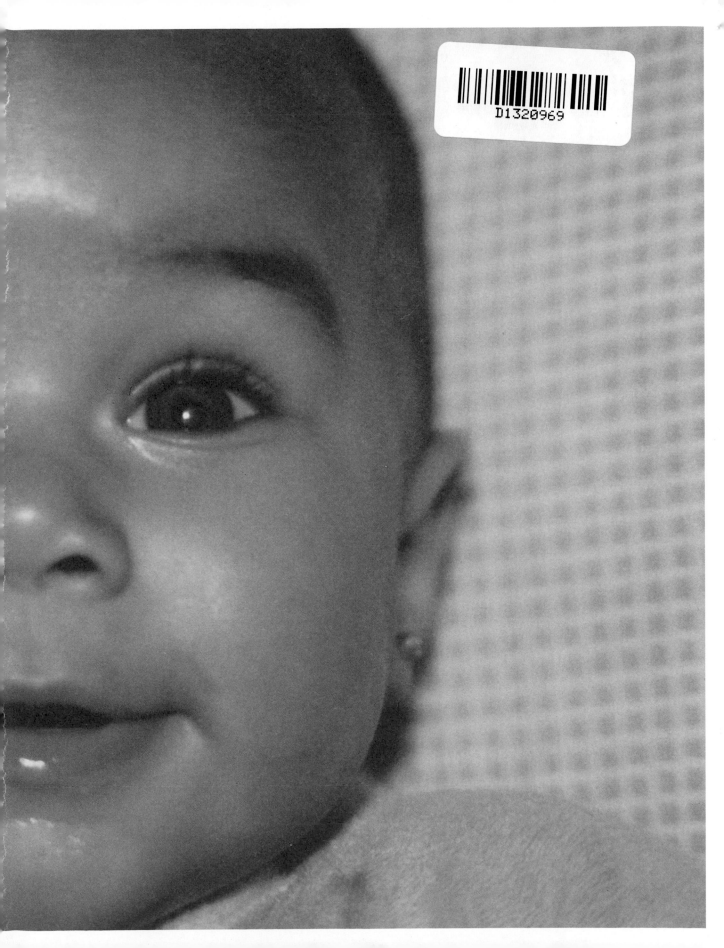

First published in Great Britain in 2009 by Hodder & Stoughton
An Hachette UK company

1

Copyright © Leona Lewis 2009
Photography / Text copyright © Leona Lewis 2009
Photography by Dean Freeman
Creative direction / concept by Dean Freeman
Designed by Joby Ellis
Cover photograph: Dress by Hervé Léger by
Max Azria at Matches, Jewellery by Laura Lee

A CIP catalogue record for this title is available from the British Library.

Hardback ISBN 978 0 340 91899 9
Trade paperback ISBN 978 0 340 99371 2

Typeset in Univers LT
Printed and bound in Italy by Graphicom Srl

Hodder & Stoughton policy is to use papers that are natural, renewable
and recyclable products and made from wood grown in sustainable forests.
The logging and manufacturing processes are expected to conform to
the environmental regulations of the country of origin.

Hodder & Stoughton Ltd
338 Euston Road
London NW1 3BH

www.hodder.co.uk

HODDER &
STOUGHTON

LEONA LEWIS

DREAMS

PHOTOGRAPHY AND CREATIVE DIRECTION BY DEAN FREEMAN

THE JOURNEY BEGINS

'Tonight eight million people have voted and here's the result. The winner of The X Factor 2006 is... Leona!'

I covered my face with my hands and bowed my head, trying to take in what I had just heard. Could it really be true? I just couldn't believe it. Ray Quinn, the runner-up, was standing beside me; suddenly he gave me a big hug and lifted me into the air. Simon Cowell rushed up on stage and threw his arms around us. Then Kate Thornton announced that I was the first woman ever to win *The X Factor*. But still it didn't sink in. Had I really won?

'As the winner of that one million pound recording contract, Leona, you're now a *bona fide* superstar pop star,' Kate said, a little while later. 'How are you feeling?'

I didn't know what to say. How could I express all the different emotions I was experiencing? I was shocked, relieved, grateful, over the moon and desperate for a hug from my mum. So many different thoughts and feelings were rushing through my head as I looked out at the audience. People were on their feet applauding me and shouting my name; it was unbelievable, just unreal. Kate Thornton's words swirled around my head. A record contract! After years of waiting and hoping, finally I had a record contract! Searching for my parents' faces in the crowd, I saw them waving madly in my direction. Then I looked over at Simon Cowell and he beamed a smile back at me. I felt dizzy with happiness.

It was such a surprise to win. It was incredible! I hadn't expected it at all. In the beginning, I didn't even think that I would get through the first audition, so I was amazed when I kept getting further and further. It was like living in a fairytale. I often felt like pinching myself to make sure it was really happening. As the weeks flew by, I didn't dare to believe that I might have a chance of winning, although I couldn't help dreaming, of course. And now it had actually happened!

Close to tears but unable to stop smiling, out of breath and totally lost for words, all I managed to blurt out was, 'I'm speechless!'

'Well, while you try and find a few words, we've got a bit of a moment for you,' Kate continued. 'We're going to cross over now to the CD factory and Andi Peters, because your debut single is about to go into production. Andi!'

My heart pounded as Andi Peters appeared on the monitor. 'Hey, it's a fantastic result. Congratulations, Leona! Well done. And this is it, the moment you've been waiting for all your life.'

He pointed at a screen showing a circular design with my name written across it. I gasped. My first single!

He was right – I *had* been waiting for this moment my whole life.

'That is what your CD looks like,' Andi said. 'And I'm going to press the button that will get your first ever single made, in 5-4-3-2-1… and there we go! Leona, your single is now being pressed.' The machines in the CD factory in Blackburn began to buzz and whirr.

'Wow!' I thought. 'It's actually happening. I really do have a record coming out!' I felt like screaming with excitement. Twenty seconds later, Andi held up the first copy of 'A Moment Like This', my debut single.

I felt completely overwhelmed. I had dreamed about putting a record out so many times! I still didn't know whether to laugh or cry. My eyes filled with tears; laughter bubbled up inside me.

'Thank you so much!' I said. 'This is a dream come true!' I looked out at the studio audience of cheering people. I felt so, so grateful to them and all the people who had voted for me over the weeks. 'You've all made my dreams come true. Thank you so much!'

'I've won!' I thought. 'Wow!' But there wasn't time to stop and think. Now I had to focus for my finale performance of 'A Moment Like This', which would round off the show; somehow I had to get through it without breaking down. Luckily, I calmed down as I started to sing and soon I forgot about everything except the music.

Then, right at the end of the song, the other *X Factor* finalists joined me on stage for the last chorus. It was really moving and the emotion finally got to me. All the tension of the past few weeks rose up inside me and threatened to burst out in huge, choking sobs. But I couldn't let it out, not there, on stage! Wait until the show is over, I told myself, and then you can cry. Somehow I managed to keep going through the last few lines of the song.

Still there wasn't time to take it all in. As soon as I came off stage I was caught up in a whirlwind. We went straight off to film the follow-up show, *The Xtra Factor*, and after that there was a massive press conference.

People kept asking me, 'How does it feel to win *The X Factor*?'

'Amazing!' I said, in a daze. 'Just incredible! I can't believe it!'

I knew that it would only feel real when I finally got home to my family. I had been away from home for what felt like ages, staying in a house with the other finalists in my group. None of us were allowed to go and see our families and I had felt really homesick. So now I just wanted to get back to Hackney and celebrate with the people I loved most. But it turned out that I couldn't go. There wasn't time, because the next morning I had to get up at the crack of sparrows to do interviews.

I felt pretty upset, but thankfully I managed to have a few moments with my family before I was whisked off to a hotel in the centre of London with Ray and two chaperones. Then I had about two hours' sleep before it was time to get up.

The week that followed was crazy busy, packed with shows, photo shoots and interviews. I rushed from one place to the next, answering questions, changing outfits and doing photo shoots. It was amazing, but life was so hectic that I didn't have a chance to absorb it all. My schedule was packed; every minute was accounted for, from the instant I woke up to the moment I went to bed.

Then, on the third day after I'd won *The X Factor*, I saw the video of 'A Moment Like This' playing in a hotel a few hours away from London. It was only the second time I had seen it since we had filmed it in a theatre in London the week before. I watched, amazed. Was that really me? It just seemed unbelievable. I had struggled for so long to achieve my goals that it was taking time for everything to sink in.

The performance part of the video was cut with montage of clips showing me getting through all the different stages of the competition, from the first audition to the finals. Seeing it again, I burst into tears. It was an amazing achievement, but at the same time I was overwhelmed by it.

'Wow,' I thought, 'this whole year has gone past in a flash and now they've put it into three and a half minutes on a video!' It was just crazy to see, a surreal experience.

I couldn't stop crying, especially at the clips showing all my family hugging me. Watching those scenes again made me realise that it wasn't just me - everyone who had ever encouraged my dreams of doing music was a part of this, from my mum and dad, my brothers, my aunt and cousins, my boyfriend and all my friends to my lovely grandmother Queenie in hospital.

'I need see my family!' I said. 'I don't care if I have to travel for five hours; I have to celebrate this with them. They're the ones who have supported me through this whole thing.'

That night I finally got to go home and celebrate properly. At last I got to hug my mum. That's when it hit me: 'Wow, Leona, you won the whole show! You won the whole thing! Do you even know what's going on right now?' And I started crying all over again.

It took a while to digest that people had been voting for me every single week until I'd won *The X Factor* – and then they had downloaded and bought the song so that it went to the Christmas Number 1. So many people had seen me getting up there every week: they had gone through the whole experience with me. The fact that they were really connecting with me seemed incredible.

That night I thought back over the years, remembering the highs and lows of my journey to *The X Factor*. How far back did the story go? Could it be traced right back to before I could even talk, when I used to sing along to my dad's music in the back of the car? Dad says he used to turn the music down only to hear a little voice pipe up behind him, 'Eee, eee, eee!'

He'd turn the music back up and then turn it down and there I'd go again, trilling away at the age of one. I vividly remember singing in the car throughout my childhood: that back seat was my first stage. Aretha Franklin, Stevie Wonder and Minnie Riperton were just some of my early favourites.

I come from an amazing family. My mum and dad have always been there for me; they've supported me every step of the way. They've had really interesting lives and done all sorts of things over the years. They used to own shops: my dad became a youth worker and later a youth offending officer; my mum started off teaching ballet and then she went into fashion designing. Later, in her thirties, she studied for a degree and became a social worker. They've travelled quite a bit and I've been all over the place with them: to New York and other parts of the States, to Pakistan and Europe.

Any time I need advice I go to my dad. He's strong and ambitious: I think I inherited a bit of that from him. He's supportive but very realistic with it, so that's kind of rubbed off on me as well. He taught me to be positive but level headed about the future.

I think I take after my mum more than my dad, though. My mum is more of a dreamer and she's quite emotional. All my life, she has said to me: 'You can do anything you want to do.' From an early age she gave me faith that I could achieve whatever I put my mind to.

Mum does whatever she wants to do; she doesn't let anyone stop her and I admire her for that. She doesn't take any notice if someone says, 'Why are you doing that?' or 'You can't do that!' She follows her passions; I've got a bit of that, too. Mum was a country girl who grew up in Wales; she was always jumping on horses and galloping around bareback. She's just very, very cool.

Like Mum, I adore animals, especially horses, and I'd love to have my own horse one day. I usually find riding incredibly peaceful, but a few months back, I was riding around the arena at a nearby stables and my horse went a bit crazy. I almost fell off, so it was really scary.

My mum was standing there watching. Afterwards, my instructor said to her, 'You must have been so frightened!'

'No,' Mum said. 'I knew she was going to be fine. You have to experience scares like that if you're going to improve. I learned to ride without reins or saddles, so I knew she would be safe.'

I was like, 'Mum, you're a bit crazy!'

I have two brothers: Bradley is three years older than I am and Kyle is two years younger. Being the only girl in the middle meant that I had to be a little bit tough when we were growing up, but my brothers and I are really close and we've always been able to confide in each other. It's been good for them to have a sister, too!

When we were little, Kyle and I really looked up to Bradley. He was so cool and always joking and making us laugh. We used to jump into his bed and he'd tell us the funniest stories: we'd stay up all night giggling. I always felt protected by both of my brothers, and I'm so proud of them.

My cousin Yasemin has always been like a big sister to me, always there for me with advice or when I was broken hearted. She knows exactly what to say to make me feel better! I'm so grateful to have her in my life. We met our friend Aysha when we were very young, and shared a passion for performing arts from the start. I admire Aysha's confidence and charisma so much: she is the greatest friend anyone could wish for and I see her as my family. I'm lucky to have such amazing people around me.

I also feel lucky to have grown up in Hackney, because it's a melting pot of cultures and people from different ethnic backgrounds. I grew up with a real mix of friends; I had Turkish and Greek friends, Chinese and Indian friends, black, white, everything. Having a broad experience of different cultures from an early age has made me a more open and cultured person than I might have been if I'd grown up somewhere more remote, so I'm very grateful for that.

I'm a real mix myself, too. My mum's got Welsh, Italian and Irish blood in her; I have roots in Guyana through my dad; and I even have Chinese heritage on my grandfather's side. I feel fortunate to have a connection with so many nationalities, because it means I can identify with a lot of different places and people. Still, I'm definitely British – I was born here and I'm proud of where I grew up and where I come from.

Like a lot of kids, I always loved music and singing. When I was nine, I started having singing lessons. Janet Edwards, my singing teacher, instilled in me a solid foundation in classical music and that led to a total love of opera. In fact, at first I wanted to be an opera singer! It was only later that I started experimenting with modern and contemporary music, jazz and blues, and as I got older, I got into rock and indie.

I love any music that moves me, but opera was definitely my first passion. My favourite opera is *Lakmé* by Léo Delibes, and 'The Flower Duet', which is best known as the British Airways theme tune, is one of my favourite songs. I also love listening to Leontyne Price and Andrea Bocelli.

It didn't occur to me to wonder whether I was good or bad at singing when I was a child: I just really enjoyed it. Then, when I was ten, my school took part in a massive concert at Wembley Arena in aid of the British Heart Foundation. Amazingly, I was picked to sing a solo part in a duet with another girl, backed by a choir. The song was an old hit from 1967 called 'Grocer Jack'. It really took me by surprise that someone had decided to give me this big chance to perform at a major event. 'Maybe I actually can sing!' I thought.

Singing was one thing; going out on stage in front of thousands of people and performing was something else altogether. But, funnily enough, I wasn't anywhere near as nervous as I would be today. Perhaps it's easier when you're a kid. 'Oh, it's a bit scary,' I thought, and then I skipped out on stage to do my thing. I sang my part and then we went into a dance routine; the audience went crazy. They loved the fact that the concert was so big and we were so small.

I was still very young, too young to be really serious about making a career out of music. I was just a little girl who loved singing, ballet and horses. Three years later, though, something much more significant happened when I entered an under-18s talent competition at the Hackney Empire. The song I chose to sing was the Celine Dion ballad, 'Heart Will Go On', which was a very ambitious number for a thirteen-year-old! I was the youngest contestant in the competition, so I was thrilled when I got through the first heat.

The memory of doing my hair and picking out my outfit for the final still really stands out in my mind. I wore black trousers and black patent shoes and a white chiffon shirt with a black and white top underneath. Looking back, it was quite a weird choice, but it felt right at the time!

Unlike at Wembley, this time I was very, very nervous before I went on stage. My legs felt like jelly and I was sick with nerves. The auditorium seemed huge and intimidating; I didn't dare look out at the audience. It felt like a really big deal because my mum's family had come down from Wales to watch me and my brothers and aunt and cousins were out there, along with loads of friends and other relatives.

Mum gave me a hug and wished me luck just before I stepped out on to the massive Hackney Empire stage. The music started and I opened my mouth to sing. I don't remember much more about the actual performance, but it must have gone well, because I won the competition! The prize was a trophy and two hundred pounds. It was the most money I'd ever seen in my life.

After the show, several producers and music industry people gave their cards to Dad, and he got a lot of calls in the next few weeks. That's when it all started rolling, really; it was such an important moment, because lots of people suddenly wanted to work with me. I began to perform more often and I started going into the studio.

I was lucky enough to go to the Brit School in Croydon, which is Britain's only free performing arts and technology school. I loved it there; it's such a creative place that encourages individual talent. I really enjoyed studying music and I gained a lot of studio knowledge. The performance aspect was there too, but we focused more on the theory side of things.

My musical background helped as well. There are lots of musical strands in my family and the performing arts are strongly represented. My dad loves music and he's created beats for as long as I can remember. Once upon a time, we simply had a little closet at home where Dad kept all his vinyl records and DJ-ing equipment. Then we moved into a house where there was enough space for a little music room in the basement, where Dad kept his records and decks. First, I recorded on eight-track and then we went on to install our first computer and our first keyboard.

As soon as he got the computer, I was like, 'Hey, I want to learn how to work it now!' The first programme we had was Cubase, which is a bit old-school now. It was really cool at the time, though, and I was on it immediately. The great thing was that it could record sounds directly onto the computer. My dad used to record me - and then we bought our mics. First we had normal handheld mics and then we upgraded to proper studio recording mics, which was brilliant. As time went on the studio grew and we kept getting new equipment, so we built a shed outside and moved the studio in there. It was a really cool set-up.

My dad's sister Laurette loves music as much as he does. She's an African drummer and she runs a charity for disabled children who learn and progress through drumming and dance. Laurette has always been very supportive of my music. She's a great lady, a very caring person, and she's always been there for me. She's got two great children as well; I'm close to both of them and they're a big part of my life. They are Dyonne, 21, who is studying drama, and Dean, 19, who's a really talented music producer. Dean and I spent a lot of time in my dad's little studio, making beats and writing and recording music that I would sing and he would produce.

Having a home studio was really handy and it taught me so, so much about the recording process. This meant that when I first started going into professional studios, people were impressed by the fact that I understood the way records are layered and mixed. 'Oh, you've had studio experience, then,' they'd say. It helped me so much.

When I was seventeen, there came a point when I started thinking to myself that school wasn't really for me anymore. I was doing well, but I kept missing lessons to go into the studio. The truth was that I was desperate to get out into the world, into the midst of things. I wanted to concentrate on doing my thing and getting a record deal, so I had to make a decision: either focus on my studies at school or dedicate myself to going into the studio.

First, I had to tell my parents that I was thinking of leaving school. They were supportive, but they said, 'Make sure it's definitely what you want to do.' I took their advice and thought hard about it until I was sure. Life would be much more difficult, I knew, but I was determined to give it a try. I wanted a record deal so much! So I left school and started working at the Pizza Hut across the road from where I lived. It wasn't something I really enjoyed, but it was practical because it was so close to home – and earning money, however little, meant I could spend time in the studio.

I mostly worked the closing shift at Pizza Hut and it was my job to clean up after everyone had left. To make the work more enjoyable, I used to turn the music up as loud as it would go and sing along and dance as I mopped the floor. I'm sure that the people walking past thought I was a bit crazy. 'Who's that mad girl dancing around with a wet sponge and a mop?' But I didn't care. The job was just a way to get by so that I could follow my dream.

I tried to get a record deal for a long time, doing the rounds on the pub and club circuit, playing gigs with an acoustic guitarist and sometimes an acoustic bassist. I was passionate about my music and worked hard writing songs, practicing my vocals and recording with my cousin and some producer friends, but it's very difficult to get signed.

Along the way, I came across so many talented people. I used to play at a small club in west London where there was a really amazing girl who played guitar and sang. 'Why hasn't she got a record deal?' I'd think. There were others, too. 'Why isn't anyone signing these people?' I wondered. Unfortunately, no one had the money to put into developing artists. You had to develop yourself.

Two years down the line, I began to have doubts. I really enjoyed doing my music, but by then all my friends had left school and were saying, 'Yeah, we've got A levels and a B Tech and we're going to college or university!'

I wondered whether I should have stayed on at school. By now I would also have A Levels and my B Tech. Instead, it was beginning to feel like I was stuck in a bit of a rut. Two years is a long time when you're just working to get by. It was hard earning the minimum wage and being so broke that I couldn't even go shopping at Top Shop! I was always asking my mum for money. 'Mum, I need some new shoes…' She was great about it. Even when she was broke, she somehow found me a little bit of something, but I hated having to ask. I started feeling really down about it.

One night in the autumn of 2004, I was visiting some friends who had just started college in Luton. It was Freshers' Week and they dragged me into a bar, where a national karaoke competition was being held. My friends urged me to enter.

'It's just karaoke,' they said. 'Do it!'

'No, I don't want to!' I said, feeling shy.

'Go on, it will be fun.'

So I got up and sang a song; I was just messing around, really, but the judge said, 'Yeah, you're through to the next round.'

'OK,' I said, hesitantly.

He asked me write down my name and address. 'All right, then,' I thought. 'Why not?'

Not long afterwards, a letter came through the door saying, 'You've been selected to go through to the semifinals!'

How could it be that easy? I told my friends about it. 'But I don't think I'll bother,' I said.

'Do it! It'll be fun,' they insisted. 'It's a great excuse for a night out drinking.'

Whatever. I went along with it for my friends' sake, because I don't drink!

My parents and cousins came down with me and, to my surprise, it turned out to be a big, big deal. The other ten contestants were very serious about winning and a massive stage had been set up for our performances. 'OK,' I thought. 'I wasn't really prepared for this, but I'll give it a go.'

I sang 'Wind Beneath My Wings' and after everyone else had done their thing, it was announced that I'd got through to the finals. Apparently, the judge was going to be the vocal coach Carrie Grant, who is best known for her work on TV shows like *Fame Academy* and *Pop Idol*.

OK, this is quite cool, I decided – especially when I was told that there was a grand prize of £10,000 and the promise of a record deal for the winner. The money sounded fantastic, but it was the record deal I was really interested in.

I practiced hard over the next few weeks. I was set to sing two songs: 'I Will Always Love You' and Mariah Carey's 'Always Be My Baby'. I was really nervous by the time I got to the venue. The other finalists were very impressive and I was sure I wouldn't win. I later saw one of the other contestants on *Stars In Their Eyes*; she went on as Anastasia. She was really talented and seemed like a really cool girl.

I sang my songs. Then they called out three names and mine was one of them; we had to sing again. To my amazement, I won! I couldn't believe it. 'Wow, that's crazy!' I thought. Winning all that money was brilliant, and at last I was going to get a record deal! The money came through soon afterwards. I didn't go spending, though; I was determined to save it up for going into the studio. What about the record deal? I kept phoning the competition organisers: 'What's happening? Am I going to meet anyone?' 'Yes, yes,' they said, but it didn't materialise. I don't know why. They kept saying it would, but it never did. I was really disappointed. Why did people keep promising things and then not following through? Over the previous four years I had met people who had made all kinds of offers and all sorts of promises, from VIP introductions in the UK and America to record deals. But nothing ever happened. I'd had my hopes raised, only to have them dashed, time and again. There had been so many offers that came to nothing that sometimes it was hard not to start feeling cynical. 'I need to be tougher,' I thought; 'I need to develop a thicker skin.' But then each time I was let down, I couldn't help feeling devastated. Why wouldn't someone give me a proper chance? Why couldn't people keep their promises?

On the other hand, I felt I couldn't give up now. Despite my disappointment over the lack of a record contract, winning the competition had given me a real boost. It spurred me on to think that people enjoyed my singing; it restored my faith in the path I had chosen. I decided that I could actually get somewhere if I kept going for it.

Things didn't get any easier, though. I still had to do very basic jobs to get by. Soon afterwards, I started working at the British School of Osteopathy, as a receptionist. I worked through the winter on the front desk, right in front of the main entrance. Every time the doors opened, a cold blast hit me and I remember freezing my butt off. There were some quite rude customers too, which was annoying. But the staff were lovely and I used to get free osteopathy from the students, who needed someone to experiment on, so that part of it was cool. I also started writing short stories again, something I had always loved doing. It was my way of escaping the boredom of being at a desk. It made the day go much more quickly to get lost in my own world.

When I left the British School of Osteopathy, I worked at a chiropodist's, again as a receptionist, which was interesting. It was just down the road from home and the hours were good, so I had quite a bit of free time to go into the studio. I was still working hard on my music and playing gigs. I refused to give up.

By then, I'd got to know the music industry a little better, although I'm still learning today. There are good and bad sides to it – you have to take the rough with the smooth. On the down side, there are some greedy, unscrupulous people on the fringes of the industry, people who want to rip you off and take you for a ride. So you have to be careful. People especially try and take advantage of you when you're a young girl, I think. I was lucky to have my dad around. He helped me check people out and took me along to meet producers at their studios, so that I didn't seem to be alone. It's important not to appear vulnerable and I was always prepared to walk away if the vibe didn't feel right.

Sometimes someone would say, 'Why don't we work together? Come to my studio and we'll do some tracks.'

'Dad, what do you think? Should I go?' I'd ask.

Dad would call them up and go down there and check that it was all legit. A few times he came back and said, 'No, it's dodgy. Don't go.'

Neither of my parents has wanted to smother me in cotton wool, but Dad's very protective and supportive and I'm grateful for that. I wouldn't have wanted to do it all alone. Even now my dad and the rest of my family are the people I trust to give me honest opinions, no matter what.

Meanwhile, I went to an interview for yet another job that I didn't really want to do, this time as a secretary for Michael Marks, a mortgage broker in Hackney.

'Can you start now?' he asked me, about five minutes into the interview.

'From Monday, you mean?' I said.

'No, right now!' he said. 'I'm desperate for a secretary and you're perfect for the job. I don't need to interview anyone else.'

'OK!' I said. Within half an hour I was filing and answering the phone.

I was glad to get the job and be on a regular salary. The office was nice and Michael was a good boss. But I wasn't using any particularly amazing skills and it wasn't leading anywhere. 'Oh God,' I thought, 'this isn't what I want to do with the rest of my life!'

'Is my music career actually going to happen?' I wondered. 'Perhaps I should just give up.' There had been so many disappointments and broken promises, so many times I thought I was getting close to achieving my dream, only to be knocked back down again. How much longer could I keep hoping and wishing? How many more times could I cope with having my dreams trampled on? Sometimes I questioned whether I had the strength to go on believing in myself and in the future. Maybe it was finally time to call it a day and get real.

A MOMENT LIKE THIS

Perhaps some people think that one morning I woke up and thought, 'Hey, I want to sing a bit, so I'll just go on *The X Factor* and win it. Easy.' But that's not how it happened! At first, I wasn't sure whether I even wanted to try out for *The X Factor*. My boyfriend Lou was the one who suggested it.

'I don't know,' I said. 'Would it be right for me?'

By now I was feeling so down about everything, especially the way the music industry worked, that I was on the verge of going back into education. I was planning to study psychology, a subject that has always interested me. In fact, I had already submitted my course application. I definitely didn't want to be a mortgage broker's secretary forever.

'Why don't you just go along for the audition?' Lou said.

'Oh, I don't know…'

Part of me thought that I should do it, but another part of me said no, because I still wanted to get into the industry my way. Anyway, did people in the music industry take *The X Factor* seriously? It seemed to me that, apart from Will Young and Lemar, none of the contestants had gone very far with their music. So I was worried that if I went that route, I might reach a dead end.

I felt torn in other ways: although deep down I believed in myself and thought I could make it, my family had been going through a hard time after my granddad died, which had a knock-on effect of making me feel unsure about everything, especially now that my granny had fallen ill as well. I was at a really low point. I hesitated, but Lou persuaded me to apply. 'OK, I'll just go for it and see what happens,' I thought.

My first audition letter came through just before I went on holiday to Jamaica, where my auntie and uncle were getting married. The audition was scheduled for the day after I returned. But when I got home from the airport I just didn't feel up to it.

'I don't want to go!' I told Lou.

'It's totally up to you,' he said, shrugging. 'But I think you should.'

I turned it over in my mind as the day went on. I dreaded the thought of being rejected by the judges. I'd had so many disappointments already; I didn't need any more knocks to my confidence.

But then it struck me that perhaps this opportunity had been sent to me and I should grasp it. And maybe there was someone out there who really wanted to go for the audition, but didn't get the call-up. 'Don't be selfish,' I thought, 'just go for it.' So I did. Like most of the contestants, I expected to turn up and see the judges, but instead it was *The X Factor* producers who decided whether I would go through or not. I didn't rate my chances.

'I'm so fed up,' I told my mum a couple of weeks later. 'I look at all my friends and they're in their first and second years at university getting their degrees, but I'm nowhere. I can't go on like this!'

Mum's response surprised me, because I knew she was keen for me to go to university. 'Just hang on for a few more months,' she said, 'because I've got a feeling that this could be your year.'

Sure enough, I was called back for another *X Factor* audition. I went for three auditions in all and each time I thought I'd see the judges, but each time I was met by the producers! Finally, after the third time, the producers said, 'OK, next time you see the judges.' It just rolled on from there. I sang 'Over The Rainbow' my first time in front of the judges. It's a song that means a lot to me because whenever I feel low, it puts me in a good place. It's a very hopeful song; the lyrics and sentiment are just so beautiful. I love Eva Cassidy's version. She's one of my favourite singers.

When I'd finished singing, Simon Cowell and Sharon Osborne clapped. 'That's what it's all about!' Simon said.

'You've got the whole package, I think,' Louis Walsh added.

True to character, Simon immediately jumped in and tempered Louis's compliment with a little bit of criticism, but then he praised me again. I was amazed. I thought he would be much scarier and meaner than he was, so I went home feeling really happy.

The audition wasn't televised until a while afterwards. By then, I'd been working for Michael, the mortgage broker, for a few months. We got along really well, partly because he was a frustrated guitarist and we often used to sit and chat about music. But, knowing he wouldn't be very pleased to discover that there was a possibility that I might be leaving my job, I hadn't told him anything about my involvement in *The X Factor*. I really thought I could hide it from him.

I watched my first audition with my family on the Saturday night it was aired, but I didn't expect Michael to see it. It was really weird seeing myself on TV! I got a million texts after the show, all saying, 'Hey, I saw you on *The X Factor*!'

As I rushed into work the following Monday, I said, 'Sorry I'm late, Michael.'

'No doubt it's because of all the people stopping you to get your autograph,' he said, laughing.

'Yes, I saw you on *The X Factor*!'

'Really?' I said. It was beginning to seem like everyone – EVERYONE – had seen my audition.

'Please don't tell me that you're going to leave me,' he said, looking panicked. 'You're not, are you?'

'I don't know, Michael. What did you think of my audition? Do you think I'm good enough to go through?' I asked him.

'I think I should be looking for a new secretary,' he said.

'That's really sweet,' I laughed, 'but I haven't got through any of the other auditions yet.'

'OK, just let me know how it goes,' he said with a sigh.

When I got through to the stage just before the finals, I decided to give in my notice. I didn't want to have to quit suddenly if I made it through to the finals. It wouldn't have been fair to leave him high and dry. He was very good-natured about it. 'I don't want to lose you, so if you change your mind, you can come straight back,' he said. I will always be grateful to him for the support he gave me.

It was an incredible feeling to make it through to the final twelve acts, because I had been sure that I wouldn't get that far. We all stayed in a house together, which was a lot of fun. Our presence there was shrouded in secrecy at first. On TV, they were still at the boot camp stage of the auditions and it would have ruined the surprise if people found out who the finalists were, so we weren't allowed to go out without disguising ourselves in case we were spotted by the paparazzi. But photographers were always buzzing around, so we had to be really careful. That was my first experience of having to dodge guys with cameras and it felt quite weird!

At the start of the finals, Michael sent me a text saying, 'I'm still holding your position open…' He texted me every week after that, until three weeks before the final show, at which point he said, 'OK, I'm finally going to let the position go.'

'Thanks for everything, Michael,' I said. 'I really appreciate it.' He sweetly gave me his guitar case as a leaving present.

Soon afterwards, there was a section on the show where each of the remaining finalists was filmed visiting our place of work, so that the viewers could see what we were doing before we went on the show. By then there was a new secretary working for Michael. We had both moved on for good, although we still swap texts from time to time. Somehow this felt like a watershed moment: it was as if I had reached the end of an era. One phase of my life was ending and another was beginning. I felt excited at the thought of what was to come.

As I've said, we weren't allowed to go and see our families, which was really hard for me. Thankfully, though, I was given special permission to visit my gran in hospital every Sunday, which also meant that I got to go home for a few hours. Queenie, as we all called my gran, was slowly fading away, so it was really important to me that I visited her regularly.

As time went on, Queenie became really popular on the ward, partly because I was on the show. When I visited, people would shout, 'Look, it's Leona from *X Factor*!' which really tickled her. There were pictures of me taken from magazines stuck up all around her bed, and my little cousins made posters and drawings of me to go next to them. I'd sit with her as she watched the repeat of the show; I'd relive the whole experience with her. She used to get me to sign lots of autographs for everyone. So she was living the high life! I'm so glad we had those afternoons together and she got to see the show.

For the final show, she was allowed out of the hospital for an hour to film a video message to me. 'I can't believe it's you up there!' she said to the camera. 'You're doing so beautifully. You're fulfilling your dream and you've made me so proud. I love you.' Her words brought me to tears. I'm so lucky to have had such a wonderful grandmother.

Meanwhile, over at the *X Factor* studios, I was getting to know someone who would prove to be very influential in my life and career: Simon Cowell. I was on Simon's team and he was my mentor. As the various stages of *The X Factor* unfolded, I began to think he was a very cool person. I found him really easy to talk to, very approachable, and he could also be quite cheeky at times. He's got a very proud streak, too. During the finals, he was often backstage with us, wishing us luck. He was a huge support as the weeks went on.

The results show was always agony and it would be a massive relief to hear that I was safe for another seven days. Then, one week I waited and waited for my name to be read out, but every time another name was announced, it wasn't mine. I looked across at Simon. His eyes were saying, 'I can't believe this!'

'Oh no,' I thought, 'he thinks I'm going to be voted out! If Simon thinks I'm going to go, then I am going to go…'

I looked across at him again. The expression on his face said, 'This is really, really bad.'

My heart began to pound. As the moments ticked by, I began to feel more and more terrified. Although I wasn't expecting to get through to the next round, I wanted it so, so badly! I had so much more to prove! I hated the idea of having to leave the show. The thought of walking away from all that

I had achieved so far appalled me. Would I have to go back to my old job, typing and filing? 'Please say my name!' I begged silently. As the seconds stretched into what seemed like hours, it felt as though my hopes and dreams were slipping away from me, and everything I had worked so hard for was crumbling before my eyes. 'Say my name!' I begged again. 'I want to stay; I have to stay!'

Finally, my name was called. I was overwhelmed by emotion as it sank in that I had been given a chance to sing again the following week. The relief in my eyes reflected the relief in Simon's eyes, which took me by surprise. In that moment I realised that he genuinely cared about me and wanted me to go far, not just because he was my mentor, but because believed in me as a singer.

But then something happened just before the semifinals that threatened to ruin things. Over the weeks, I had been making a few small changes to the backing tracks to the songs I was singing. The instrumental part of each song was arranged by the musical director, Nigel Wright, and before every show he and I had a chat about how I wanted the next show's track to sound. Nigel went along with my suggestions and was very respectful, which I'm sure had a lot to do with the fact that I was on Simon's team.

Because of my studio experience, I was always very clear about how the instrumental should sound. 'This needs to be down in the mix,' I'd say. 'These chords need to change...' No one else even thought to question Nigel's arrangements, so it sometimes raised an eyebrow. 'Excuse me!' he'd joke, but it was never a problem.

For the semifinal in early December, I was set to sing 'Over The Rainbow' again. I originally wanted the backing track just to be acoustic guitar, because the song speaks for itself, really, and the music is simply there to support it. But it came back with all this instrumentation that was really over the top and razzy, like a big musical number. This worried me, because it's an important song to me and I really wanted it to come across well. I ran through it a couple of times, but it wasn't working for me. 'Don't worry, it's fine,' everyone said when I voiced my doubts. 'It's only a backing track. Just sing the song and it will be great.'

I wasn't convinced. 'Oh dear,' I thought. 'I'd rather not sing the song with this instrumentation, because I just don't feel the emotion in the music.' But I felt torn, because I didn't want to offend Nigel.

We were singing two songs each in the semifinal, so for a couple of days I focused on my other choice, 'I Have Nothing' by Whitney Houston. All the while, my anxiety about 'Over The Rainbow' kept buzzing around my brain. Finally I decided to go to Simon and have a chat about it. It was a last-minute decision, but I had to do it, however scary the idea seemed.

My heart was in my mouth as I went to find him. I didn't want to upset him or make him think any less of me. No one wants to rock the boat; that's why I left it to the last minute. I knocked softly on his door. Oh god, could I really go through with this? After all, he was my mentor. And he was Simon Cowell! I wondered if he'd think I was being difficult. Perhaps he'd tell me to stop complaining and send me away.

'Come in!' I heard him say. My hand trembled as I turned the handle and pushed open the door. I fought back the urge to run away. Like it or not, this had to be done.

'Yes, how can I help?' he asked.

'Simon, this song is really important to me,' I explained, a bit shakily. 'The music behind it has to be really special and really complement the song,' I went on. 'It has to be emotional and I'm not feeling it.'

He sat down and listened to the track. 'I totally see what you mean,' he said. 'Let's get it changed. I don't care how long it takes or what we have to do. You tell them exactly what you want and we'll get it done, even if it takes all night.'

I was really impressed. Everyone else had been saying, 'Just stick with the music. Just do it,' whereas Simon seemed to understand how much the song meant to me. I have a lot of respect for him for listening. I'll never forget what he said next: 'Always follow your instincts. You've got great musical instincts and you should never be afraid to speak your mind.'

'Don't worry, we'll change it,' Nigel said. He wasn't in the slightest bit offended, even when I said it still wasn't right after it came back a second time. This was quite late in the day, but I wanted it to be perfect. I was glad that I'd been able to be honest about it. I had always known my own mind when it came to music, but I think this was the moment that Simon saw me as a proper artist. He recognised that I had a strong sense of what I wanted to do, the sound I wanted and how I wanted to be portrayed. It was also a turning point because it became clear that Simon and I understood each other musically. I had a lot of confidence afterwards, in myself and in him.

It was around this time that I started to get fan mail and presents in the post. I couldn't believe my eyes when I read letters that started with the words, 'Dear Leona, I really love your singing, your songs and your voice.'

'Wow!' I thought. You know you're reaching people when they've taken the time and effort to write a letter and pour all their feelings into it. Sometimes it felt a bit surreal, but often I was really touched by the things people wrote. Some of them talked about being moved by my interpretation of a particular song that meant a lot to them, which really made me happy. A lot of people seemed to love my version of 'The First Time Ever I Saw Your Face', which is a very special song for me, so I was thrilled that people liked what I had done with it. I'm always really pleased when people tell me that my music has reached them in some way: that's what it's all about for me. It feels incredibly fulfilling when someone tells me that they've played one of my songs at their wedding, or at a christening or a family party or anniversary. The thought that my music means that much to them is amazing.

Things were changing fast, and not just for me. I guess it must have been strange for my parents to see me on TV every week and in the papers, because I'm just Leona, their daughter. But they took it in their stride. They're very cool parents! It was so, so amazing when I finally got to go home and spend some time with them after I had won, when the initial whirlwind was over. 'Yes, I did it, you did it, we did it!' we screamed at each other. I could tell they were really proud of me, especially when we heard that 'A Moment Like This' had been downloaded at a record-breaking rate. First, the family celebrated and at a later date we had a big party. I invited all my friends, the people who had supported me through the show and some of the other X Factor contestants. It was a really brilliant night.

There was a break of ten days before the next whirlwind started and Simon Cowell very kindly paid for me and my family to have what he called 'a well earned rest' in Dubai, which was lovely and relaxing. It was quite sunny, so we did a lot of swimming. One day we actually went skiing at an indoor ski resort, which had real snow and massive slopes. It was like being in the Swiss Alps, which was very weird!

When we got back, I went straight into planning my album, *Spirit*. I wanted to take my time over it; I was determined not to rush it or release anything that I wasn't happy with. But would that be possible? I had heard stories about record companies putting pressure on artists to release stuff before they were ready. Thankfully, Simon totally supported me. 'However long it takes to make a great album, that's how long we'll wait for your album to come out,' he told me. 'Just take as much time as you need.' His words would prove to be very reassuring during the difficult months to come.

He had in mind some of the producers that he wanted me to work with and we both knew the direction I wanted to go in, so we worked well together. I wasn't totally fixed in my approach, though. One thing I knew for sure was that I definitely wanted to record some classic, ballad-type songs with a modern sound and a 1980s feel to them. It was all about the big songs – and then we could work on the production around them.

Classic songs will always be the core of what I do, but I was also open to going slightly rock, having more of a band sound behind me or getting into a rhythm and blues vibe. Don't get me wrong, I'd never want to do 'a bit of this, a bit of that.' I have a sense of where I want to go. But I don't think you should necessarily stick to one thing all the time. You should try different things out. You shouldn't stifle your creativity.

'By the way,' Simon said next. 'Clive Davis wants to meet you. He wants to be involved.'

Clive Davis! What, *the* Clive Davis? The legendary producer and record company executive, the founder of Arista Records and J Records, the force behind the musical careers of artists from Janis Joplin and Santana to Whitney Houston? And that's not even a miniscule part of who Clive Davis is and how momentous he is to the music industry!

'OK,' I said lightly, but I didn't believe him, because it couldn't be true. I thought he must be joking. But then I got a call from Clive Davis's A&R people! They wanted to meet me! And at the meeting they told me that, yes, Clive Davis really did want to be involved in the making of my album, and he really did want to meet up with me. It was just incredible.

I flew to America to meet Clive at the Beverley Hills Hotel, where he was staying in the run-up to the Grammy Awards – America's biggest annual music awards. I felt pretty intimidated as I made my way to his hotel bungalow, which is his second home and where he conducts all his West Coast business. 'What will he think of me?' I wondered. He's worked with and influenced some of the greatest artists of the last forty years, including some of my idols, so I wasn't sure how he would react to me. I hoped that I wouldn't get too nervous when I met him. It was a huge deal that he had expressed an interest in working with me, so I couldn't help but feel a little bit anxious as I made my way through the hotel. What if he changed his mind when he met me? I was expecting him to be some majorly scary dude and I was really worried that I'd get tongue-tied. But, as it turned out, Clive is a very sweet, nice person and he couldn't have been more welcoming. Plus, he's got a really cute dog called Teddy. Of course, I couldn't help making a fuss of Teddy, holding him and stroking him, so that kind of broke the ice.

Clive was very precise about how he wanted to help me, how he would be involved and what he wanted me to do. He asked me to sing for him in his front room, which was quite scary, but he was just lovely and really supportive, so it wasn't half as bad as it could have been. His plan was to showcase my singing on the day before his pre-Grammy party, which is something of an event these days, to put it mildly. The showcase would serve as an introduction. It would be a case of, This Is The Girl! and he explained that he was going to invite along lots of different songwriters to hear me sing and meet me. That way they would get a vibe from me and we would take it from there. Hopefully, some of them would want to write songs for me.

Wow! I was so, so flattered, because he had only ever done this for one artist before and that was Whitney Houston, one of my all-time heroes. It was amazing that he was going to do the same for me. And Ne-Yo was coming! It was a lot of pressure, though. I was so nervous before I went on, and I don't think people realise how much nerves can hinder your performance. Your breathing becomes shallow, so you can't hold your notes properly and you can't support your voice properly, so it does really affect the way you sing.

Before the showcase, I hid in the ladies' loos feeling so sick and shaky that I didn't think I'd be able to go on stage. 'What if I mess up in front of everyone?' I thought. It was absolutely terrifying. I was singing three songs: 'Over The Rainbow', 'Summertime' and a song I had already recorded for the album. I made a wobbly start. It was excruciating. I couldn't get over the fact that some of the best songwriters in the world were watching me. Still, I needed to pull myself together quickly. 'OK, just calm down,' I told myself. 'Remember that all these people have seen you sing before. They must have done – otherwise they wouldn't have come to the showcase, would they?' At the very least, they would have gone on to YouTube to check me out. 'You've got one shot, just give it your best,' I thought.

By the second song I was properly into my flow and ready to go. On some level, I could sense the atmosphere in the room relax as I found my voice and began to lose myself in the song. It was a huge relief. I've since learned that it's OK to get nervous before the show but, seriously, when you get out on stage, you just have to turn it off. These days I know how to get lost in the song and forget about everything else, but back then, it was all new to me and I was filled with trepidation.

I remember an interviewer once asked me, 'What colour do you see when you sing?' No one had ever asked me that before and it made me think, because colours are very poignant to me when I sing. Focusing on a colour is a way of evoking the emotion from a song and transporting myself into my own world. There are different colours for different moods and occasions. If I'm singing a happy song, I'll probably see pastel pinks. With something more poignant, I'll see darker blues and deep colours.

My next big challenge was the *X Factor* tour. It was a really big deal: thirty-two dates in massive arenas up and down the country, with only two days off in more than a month! It was a very daunting thought, but I didn't realise quite how intimidating I would find it until I arrived at the Metro Radio Arena in Newcastle in the middle of February, the day before the opening show.

Up until then, I had been rehearsing in London at little dance studios around the capital. So I couldn't wait to get up on stage and do it for real, or so I thought. It would be great to get a proper sense of the whole production, finally. I was set to come on last and sing five songs: 'Could It Be Magic'; 'Sorry (Seems To Be The Hardest Word)'; 'A Moment Like This'; 'Over The Rainbow'; and 'I Will Always Love You'.

I got on a train to Newcastle, fluttering with nerves and excitement. Thankfully, I was with Nicola Carson, from my management company. Nicola and I clicked from the first time we met, during *The X Factor*. She's an amazing person and I instantly felt a connection with her. Our working relationship – and, alongside that, our friendship – just blossomed from there. It's hard to explain: it's as though we were somehow meant to meet and be a part of each other's lives.

I'd realised that Nicola was definitely going to be an important part of my life just a few days after I won the show. Everyone was running around sending me here and there, while inside all I wanted to do was see my family and I was quite upset and down about it. I should have been overjoyed and excited, but we had been apart for so long – throughout the show – that I was feeling extremely lonely and homesick. I was suddenly surrounded by all these people I didn't know and I felt isolated in the midst of them all, because I had no one to talk to. I tried to cover it up, because I just wanted to make everyone happy, but Nicola immediately sensed what was wrong. She told everyone to calm down and announced that I must go home and be with my family. She always looks out for me.

When I arrived in Newcastle, I made my way to the arena in time for the afternoon's big production rehearsal. It sounds crazy, but I just wasn't prepared for how enormous the venue was. The stage was gigantic! I looked out at the auditorium and gulped as I imagined how it would look when it was packed with thousands of people. Just the thought made me dizzy. The pressure was on.

Now I had to listen hard and take in all my stage directions, which were really quite complicated. It wasn't just a case of going out there and singing the songs. For the first number, I would be rising up out of the floor on a platform. Later in my set I had to walk slowly down a flight of steps swirling with dry ice – without falling over. That was the hard bit. Walking down those steps was a lot more difficult than it appeared to be. They were very steep, so I kept looking down in case I lost my footing. 'Don't look down!' someone shouted. 'Keep your eyes on the audience.' I tried again, but by now the dry ice was misting up the bottom steps and I couldn't see a thing. I had real trouble keeping my balance, because it felt like I was stepping down into a cloud of nothing. To make things worse, people were shouting instructions from all sides. It really put me off my singing. I thought I sounded terrible and I probably looked pretty shaky as well.

After running through it a couple of times, I still wasn't getting it. 'Oh no,' I thought. 'This is a disaster! I'm going to make a complete idiot of myself in front of thousands of people.' I couldn't help myself: I walked off the back of the stage, found a dark corner and burst into tears.

Nicola came to find me. 'What's wrong?' she asked.

All my fears came out in a jumble of words and sobs. 'I'm so scared!' I told her. 'I don't want to let anyone down. I'm worried about my voice holding up and all the dry ice is putting me off!'

'Let's have a break,' she said. 'We need to talk this through.'

We went back to the dressing room for a cup of tea and a chat. 'If the dry ice is a problem, we'll get rid of it,' Nicola said. 'Nobody's coming to see dry ice. They're coming to see you. So we'll do whatever it takes to make sure that we can put on a great show and you can feel good about it.'

Her words reassured me, but I still felt anxious. So many people had spent their hard-earned money on tickets to this show, after voting for me week after week. What if I couldn't pull it off? It would be a huge let down, not only for the audience, but for all the people working on the show, from the riggers and the roadies to the stage managers. As the winner of *The X Factor*, there was a lot riding on my performance. Nothing could be worse than failing to live up to that. I couldn't fail! And I was determined not to. I had to rise to the occasion and be professional. 'Come on!' I told myself. 'Pull yourself together. You can do it!' I thought about how long I'd worked for an opportunity like this, how many times I had dreamed of performing in front of thousands of people. 'This is it,' I thought. 'Make it good!'

I went on psyching myself up until I felt ready to go back to the stage for another try. This time, my voice sounded fine and I made it down the steps without looking down – or, more importantly, without tumbling down to the bottom and breaking a limb.

'Well done, Leona,' Nicola said, beaming at me. 'You killed it!' Everyone else seemed really pleased as well. I breathed a sigh of relief.

My confidence was back. Now it was time to focus on the details. I took another look at the dresses I was set to wear on stage. 'They're not glittery enough!' I told Nicola. 'They definitely need some sparkle.'

'You're right,' she said. We rushed out to a local haberdashery shop and bought a mountain of diamanté; we spent every free hour after that glueing little crystals on to my dresses.

The next day there was a full dress rehearsal and then it was the opening night of the show! I was nervous before I went on, but it helped having familiar faces around backstage, especially Ray, Nikitta, Ashley and the MacDonald Brothers. And it wasn't like it was a solo show, so there was lots of support. We had a real laugh backstage and Ash was always cracking jokes, which took the edge off.

All the same, my knees felt weak as I waited below the stage for the cue that would signal the start of my opening number. Then suddenly it was time to go. As I rose up through the floor to reach stage level, the noise of the audience increased until it was a deafening wall of shouting and screaming. I looked breathlessly out into the auditorium. The whole place was going crazy. It was totally, totally amazing.

TOUGH TIMES

Being on *The X Factor* tour made me feel like I had achieved something incredible. It was so amazing to be there on stage in front of people who had paid to see the show and wanted to see me perform. It was a real contrast to the gigs I'd done at pubs and clubs, where there was an audience simply because people had come out for a drink that night, where people didn't know who I was and didn't necessarily care.

It was completely different to playing in small clubs and venues in another way, too. You have to give much more in those big arenas than you would in a smaller, more intimate venue, where people can get a feel for you more easily because they're closer to you. You have to find a way to reach the people everywhere in the arena, because you want them to feel the emotion that everyone at the very front can feel. Each and every person should feel involved, a part of the show, so you have to throw your energy right around the whole place. It means connecting to a huge number of people – and that can make it quite a draining experience.

I started the tour with an adequate amount of rehearsal under my belt, but my performance definitely developed during the weeks that followed. Since I'm not a natural talker and I get tongue-tied very easily, especially if I'm nervous, at first I very much stuck to a plan when it came to what I said and did on stage. Then, as time went on and I became more comfortable, I started to mix things up a bit. I tried out different ways of singing each song and moving to it, and I experimented with how I introduced the songs and the things I said in between them. When I found that something worked, I tended to stay with it, but I got rid of anything less successful and tried something else the next night. So it was a real learning curve!

After playing in Aberdeen, Nottingham, Sheffield, Birmingham, Manchester, Glasgow, Brighton and Cardiff, I was really looking forward to getting back to London and playing at Wembley. Having performed there once as a child, it was a thrill to come back and do a solo performance as the winner of the show. Plus, the tour schedule had been totally crazy and at last I was going to have a day off, which meant that I would be able to go home. I couldn't wait to be with my family again.

But when I arrived in London the day before the Wembley show, it transpired that my grandmother was very, very ill, and my family was with her at the hospital. I was absolutely distraught. However, I was very thankful that I was able to go and see her. A few days earlier and I would have been in Wales; a few days later I would have been in Ireland, unable to break away from the tour. To me, this was not a coincidence. There was definitely something about it that was meant to be. I was supposed to see her one last time and I would have felt terrible if I hadn't been able to.

It was really hard going to the hospital. I felt so sad. I loved my gran so much. On the other hand, she was very old and she had never recovered from my granddad's death. She was definitely dying of a broken heart as well as old age. She and my granddad had been the glue that kept the family together. They were a really amazing couple and she had been very lonely without him. I saw her a few days before she died. When the news came through that she had passed, I went to the hospital again. The whole family was in pieces.

That night, I was due to perform at Wembley. It was going to be the biggest show of the tour. 'I can't do it,' I told my dad, in floods of tears. I couldn't imagine going on stage as if nothing had happened.

'I understand,' Dad said gently. 'But she would have wanted you to do it, you know…'

He was right. I thought back to all those Sundays when Queenie and I had watched the repeat of *The X Factor* together in the hospital ward; I remembered how proud and happy she had been to watch me, how I had signed autographs for her to give out to other patients and visitors. So the last thing my grandmother would have wanted would be for me to miss my most important show. Somehow I got myself together and made my way to Wembley for the sound check.

My performance that night was full of emotion, more than ever before. It was definitely different to any other performance that I'd given. It was a bittersweet occasion, because Wembley was somewhere I had always wanted to perform and it was totally exhilarating to be there, but I was still trying to absorb the shock of what had happened earlier.

I was comforted by a strong sense that my grandmother was watching in some way, which she would not have been able to do if she had been alive, because she would have been too ill to come to the show. So there were all these feelings and thoughts swirling around as I went on stage and the emotion just came bursting out of me as I sang. I'll never forget how that felt. It was a totally memorable night.

The tour was tough going at times. We had to work hard and there was no time off between gigs for most of it. I didn't mind because it gave me a taster of how things will be when I do my own tour; I feel much better prepared as a result.

As soon as it was over, I went straight into recording my album. I couldn't wait to get into the studio, because that's often where I feel most at home. I wanted to work with a mixture of writers and producers; there were some producers that I had always dreamt of working with, but I was also open to suggestion.

I jumped at the chance of working with Walter Afanasieff, or Walter A as a lot of people call him. I've always admired him and he's written some of my favourite songs, including 'Heart Will Go On' and 'Anytime You Need A Friend'. He's worked with Mariah Carey, Whitney Houston, Destiny's Child, Christina Aguilera, Josh Groban... the list goes on forever.

It was incredible that I got to work with him and I felt so honoured to be in the studio with someone I admire so much, whose songs I have listened to and enjoyed, sung my heart out to and cried over. It was a dream come true to be able to say, 'Walter, can you play the piano for me, please?'

'Sure,' he'd say. While he played I'd be thinking, 'Oh my God, I can't believe I'm actually in the same room with him – and he's playing music!'

Over the course of making the album, it struck me that the people who sustain long careers in writing and producing are the ones who have stayed hungry. Diane Warren is a great example of this. I found Diane very inspiring. Name anyone – from Whitney Houston to Toni Braxton – and she's probably written one of their biggest hits. So, for the past twenty-five years, Diane has been writing the best-selling, most popular songs around, but you wouldn't know it to meet her, because she acts as if she's just coming up. She's so full of passion and enthusiasm; she never stops striving to do her best. 'Listen to this song! Do you like it?' she'd say to me.

'Hey, you're, like, the best writer in the world. What do you mean? Why are you even asking me?'

Meanwhile, my management suggested trying out relatively new producers as well. 'How about Ryan Tedder? He's very up and coming,' I was told. Well, I hadn't heard of Ryan or his band One Republic, but when he played me his music, I thought it was just awesome. I definitely wanted to give new people a chance to be heard and to get their music out there, if I could. After all, I was being given an incredible opportunity, so why shouldn't I try and pass that on? For me, making a great album wasn't just about working with the massive A list producers, although they're incredible and amazing and come up with great stuff. I also knew that there's a whole world of creativity out there to embrace and be a part of – and there are always talented new people trying to find an outlet for their material.

I'm quite lucky in that I've always known what I want to do and what direction I want to take – musically, anyway. As regards to everything else, from styling to staging, I'm quite happy to say, 'OK, what are your suggestions?' But musically I've always had a strong sense of which songs I think will work for me.

I know a lot of singers who go in the studio, sing the song and then let the producers do everything else. That's one way to do it and it's a fine way, because the singer is simply concentrating on his or her art. But I'm not like that. I like to get very involved with the mixing and the vocal comp, which makes the process a whole lot longer; it probably doubles the time, in fact. I put everything into what I do and it pays off, I think. At least, I'm pretty sure that it shows on the final mix. I do the best that I can because I don't ever want to hear one of my songs and think, 'I could have done that so much better if I had just stayed in the studio and done more!' It would be horrible to feel that.

I don't know, perhaps you could call me a control freak. I'm not sure if I would call myself one, but once I asked a producer if she thought I was and she said, 'Er, you think?' and then laughed. As if I was stating the obvious! So, maybe people do think that about me when I'm in the studio. It's funny, because I'm so the opposite to controlling in everyday life – normally I'm very easygoing. I don't know where I get it from: I just want things to be perfect! But at the same time I know that nothing can ever be perfect. So I've learned to accept that a producer is probably right when he or she says, 'That was the hundredth take, Leona. It's time to move on now.' Sometimes you have to let things go - and you may even come to realise later that the first take was the best one!

Making *Spirit* was a long, sometimes difficult and mostly enjoyable process. I had many great experiences in the studio, and only one or two bad times. I went into writing camps in various places, including Atlanta, where I worked with a load of different writers and producers. It was often a case of going into the studio and seeing what comes out. Atlanta was pretty crazy . I worked with a really great writer whose inspiration came at all different hours of the day. He would suddenly call me up and say, 'OK, come to the studio now!' So I'd get there at eight o'clock at night and stay until five in the morning. It was cool, though. It was different.

I did some good work in Atlanta, but I didn't feel I'd found the overall direction for my album yet, which worried me. OK, I was still at the very start of the process, but I didn't know if I was as far along as I should be or would like to be. That's the whole thing about the recording process, although I wasn't aware of it at the time. You have a dry patch, and then everything comes at once, so it's all about seeing how it goes.

I began to have doubts, though. I felt quite lonely and homesick and then I came down with tonsillitis, which made me feel a lot worse, because it meant I had to rest my voice and couldn't work. When you're under the weather, everything seems darker than it really is. Am I going to get the great material that I want? I started asking myself. What's going to happen? Am I doing the right thing?

In the end my throat became so bad that I had to fly home to recover. It was really depressing. 'How's it going? Did you find some great songs?' people kept asking. I wasn't sure what exactly I'd managed to achieve out there. Was it me or was it the producers I was working with? Thankfully, Simon Cowell's reassuring words about taking as long as I needed over the album were always in the back of my mind.

Because I've been in studios my whole life, I know exactly how I want my voice to sound and I like to comp and mix all my own vocals. But when you're writing with people or laying down the vocals on their songs, they also have an input into how it sounds. Still, I don't forget that I am the face and the voice of the song, so it has to represent me entirely. As a result, I don't mess around; I'm quite forward about getting my views and opinions across. It's quite difficult for me sometimes, because I'm not the kind of person who says, 'I want this! I want that!' I find it really hard to do that. But I'm passionate about my music and how I want it to sound, so I have to do what I have to do. I don't go, 'Rrroar!' I'm not a scary lady! But sometimes it may turn into a bit of a heated debate and I love that, because it shows that you're both passionate about the music.

In Atlanta I went into the studio with a producer called Novel, who is originally from the Deep South. We had a fun time. He's a really talented and cool guy. 'Right, yes, I want you to do it like this...' he'd tell me.

'OK,' I'd say, 'but I think I'm going to do it this way, actually.'

By the end, his catchphrase for me was: 'No, I think I'll do it this way.'

It used to make him laugh. He said, 'You're polite with it, but you know how to put your point across.'

I've never actually had a row with a producer, but I remember almost pulling my hair out once when I had a disagreement over a song. Although I totally got along with him outside the studio, I wasn't feeling how the producer worked or how he wanted me to come across. He was trying to make me sound very generic, always saying, 'Don't sing this note,' or 'Don't sing like that,' or 'Don't sing in that tone.'

The thing is, I sound how I sound and I don't think there's any changing it. That's what I do naturally. That's just me. I can't help it. When we came to put the song together, he decided against using a particular take 'because I don't like what's happening with your voice in that part!' He wanted the vocal to be very linear and I'm not a linear singer.

'But that's how I sound,' I said.

I'd love to be able to say who it was, but I can't, because we're good friends now. We just had completely different ideas about what we wanted to do at the time. There were moments when I thought, 'I can't work with this person!' I was on the verge of saying, 'Right, I'm going home! I don't want to sing this song.' However, I knew I had to stay because it was an amazing song...

We worked on it once, twice and then three times, until I was just getting to the point of saying, 'OK, this is it. This is the recording! That's it. We can't do this anymore!' It was about to turn into one of those songs that you can't listen to, because the process of putting it down is just so painful. It's funny to think back on it because, as it happens, it's one of my favourite songs on *Spirit*.

The thing is, we both knew it was a great song and we both wanted to get it right. But when you know you're on the brink of something great, you tend to become jittery. 'Oh gosh, is it going to work? Perhaps we should do it this way?'

'No, I think you should do it this way!'

You argue it out, and yet you know that you're only fighting because it's something you're both completely passionate about. Usually, I love thrashing out opinions. It's only when the other person becomes too controlling that I feel like walking out. Eventually we reached a compromise. I'm all for compromising, especially when someone has written the song: it's their baby and they're fired up about it. But, hey, let me do my bit, and you can do your bit!

I'm happy with the song now and so is he. He's over the moon about it, in fact. The only thing I would say is that it really comes to life for me when I sing it live, although it's great on the record too. Maybe that's because live is so much better anyway – or perhaps it's because when I sing it live I do all the things that he told me not to do!

People often ask me whether the way I sing is influenced by other people. Of course, loads of different singers have had a huge impact on me, people like Eva Cassidy, Minnie Riperton and Stevie

Wonder, the artists my parents played when I was younger. I don't sound like any of them and I can't say that I've taken anything specific from any one of them, but their influence is embedded in me and when it comes out, I just kind of make it my own.

For me, it's more about the feeling you put on certain words. Take Mariah Carey, for instance: those riffs and notes are obviously influenced by gospel music and there is somewhat of a technique to her singing, but I think it's more of a feeling than anything else. It's not something you can be taught; it's an influence you take in and express in your own way.

After Atlanta, I went to Los Angeles and spent a few months there writing with different people. It was a lonely process. People came out to visit me from London, but for the majority of the time, I was on my own. My A&R guy, Tim Byrne, was looking after me and he is so cool and I love him to bits, but I felt very much alone without my family and friends. After all, I was only 21. I was too scared to drive, because the freeway system is really complicated. But you can't walk anywhere, because no one walks in LA. It's crazy.

During the day I worked in the studio; in the evening I watched TV and movies. That was my life, for months on end. I guess it was good because I got to totally focus on my music, but I do remember feeling a little bit low sometimes. I spoke to my mum every single day, sometimes for hours at a time. Her phone bills were horrendous! I couldn't wait for my family and my friends to come over. I'd be so excited when they arrived – but of course when they left I'd feel really sad.

I also spent some time in New York, which was cool, because you can walk around there – and everything is open twenty-four-seven. That's the thing I like about America. Everything's always open. When I can't sleep, I like to go out for a wander, and New York is good for that, especially because people don't recognise me as much. I can go to Starbucks knowing that I'll be fine on my own.

The first time I recorded in New York, the record label put me up in an OK hotel – well at first I thought it was OK. It definitely wasn't great. Nicola and I booked in for three weeks and I went to the studio every day. About a week into our stay, I noticed Nicola scratching her legs. 'Have you been bitten too?' I asked, showing her my calves, which were covered in tiny insect bites.

'Yes, it must be gnats or something,' she said.

That night we got back to the hotel at around two in the morning, after a very long day in the studio. I was so relieved as I got into bed: sleep, at last! Suddenly, I saw several tiny black bug things crawling about on my sheets. 'Argh!' I yelped.

Right then, my room phone rang. 'I've got bugs in my bed!' Nicola shrieked.

'Me too!' I screamed back. 'What are they?'

'I don't know!' she said. 'Let's try Googling them.'

After an hour on the computer, we decided they were bed bugs, so we rang down to reception. Soon a couple of staff arrived to inspect the beds. 'Those are definitely not bed bugs,' they insisted.

'Either way, we're not sleeping with them,' Nicola said. 'We've been bitten all over already!'

It was five in the morning by the time we persuaded the hotel to change our rooms; we were feeling tired, depressed and itchy. It wasn't long before I had to go into the studio again.

'Just in case your beds are actually infested with bed bugs,' one of the staff told us, 'all your clothes must be washed immediately, because bed bugs lay their eggs in clothes.'

So all our clothes were sent to the hotel laundry and our suitcases were disposed of, which meant that we had nothing clean to wear the next day. In the morning we went straight to H&M and bought new outfits.

'Our hotel has bed bugs!' I told everyone at the studio.

'Really?' they said, edging away.

We had to spend another week and a half at this hotel and it was horrible. We hated every night we were there! On our last day, Nicola bought two 'I HEART NY' t-shirts and added 'EXCEPT THIS HOTEL!' using a big marker pen. She even wore hers as we walked through the lobby when we left!

As it turned out, I found the best material right at the end of the recording process. It happened a few times: just when I thought the album was done, my management company would send over a new song and it would be a case of, I just have to record this!

One morning I was in my bedroom when an email came through from them saying, 'We really like this song. What do you think?' As soon as I heard it, I thought, 'Gosh, it's really good. I want to hear it again.' In fact, I wanted to play it ten times!

When I first listen to a song, I don't hear the lyrics as much as the melody and what's going on musically. But as soon as I listened to this song again and heard the lyrics, they got stuck in my head. I took a few days over it and I found that I kept wanting to hear it again. With each listen it sounded different, somehow. It really drew me in and I knew I wanted to record it. I was sure that I could do something good with it. Other people have said, 'It took me a few times of listening to it and then I really got into it.' But I felt it instantly. So you've probably guessed by now that the song was 'Bleeding Love'!

There was a male vocal on it when I first heard it and I later found out that it was Jesse McCartney, who co-wrote the song with Ryan Tedder. I started getting to know Ryan when I went to LA to work on 'Take A Bow', which is also on the album. We worked with some of the writers he works with and then just the two of us went into the studio to work on 'Bleeding Love'.

We spent the first day just playing with different keys and trying to find the right ones. It was a nice, relaxed time because we had already got to know each other and built up a bit of a foundation. 'We're going to find the sweet spot in your voice,' Ryan said. Well, we found it! On the second day, I went into the studio and recorded it.

Ryan told me that he had sent four songs to my management company. At first, he wasn't going to include 'Bleeding Love' but at the last minute he decided to add it onto the end of the email and see what the reaction was. It's a bit scary to think that I might never have got to hear it.

When the feedback came, it was, 'No, no, no,' except for 'Bleeding Love'. 'That's really strange!' Ryan thought. 'OK, she can record it and let's see what happens.' He definitely didn't expect it to turn out how it did. But after I had recorded it, I had a call from Simon Cowell. 'I. Love. This. Song.' he said. He just knew it was going to blow up.

BREAKTHROUGH

Originally, the first single from the album was going to be 'Better In Time'. Everyone was agreed on that. Everyone except me, that is! After I recorded 'Bleeding Love', I was adamant that it should be the first release. Simon felt so too, so at the last minute we decided to make it the first single.

Simon has mentored me in a really good way; he has helped enormously with all of the song choices and picking singles. He understands music and always knows when a song is going to connect with people. He is very much seen as a businessperson, which he is; he's a really good businessman. But he's also very passionate about music, passionate about singers and he has a real ear for music. I think people forget that he has that emotional side.

Obviously the video for 'Bleeding Love' was going to be a crucial part of marketing the song, because there are so many music channels now. We needed a video that represented me and showed how I had moved on from *The X Factor*, while staying true to who I was as an artist and where I had come from. So that's not much to ask!

A lot of directors sent in their show reels for consideration and my management company whittled them down for me. Since this was my first big video shoot, it was as important to find a director I would get along with and feel comfortable with as it was to choose someone who had a great show reel.

We decided on the amazing Melina Matsoukas, because a lot of her work was very beautiful and soft. She's a young director and very cool. I wanted a video with universal appeal that everyone could relate to: something with a story, but nothing too specific. I also wanted it to be multicultural, featuring people from different ethnicities.

I was amazed when the treatment came back, because it closely resembled a short story I had written when I was working as a receptionist, which was about a girl living in an apartment block who overhears her neighbours' conversations. To the left of her apartment, a couple was always having rows; when she went into her bathroom, she'd hear the people upstairs talking through their day. Although she never met her neighbours, she knew all about their lives and the various situations they found themselves in.

Melina's idea was obviously more visual and set me in one apartment, performing the song, juxtaposed with a range of scenes going on in the apartments next door, upstairs and downstairs. Each scene would show a different situation to tie in with the lyrics of the song, so there was someone longing for love and missing love, someone being cheated on and a long lost love coming back.

'This director definitely gets me and where I'm coming from!' I thought.

When it came to shooting, I couldn't believe how much work goes into a video and how many people it takes. I arrived on set on the morning of the shoot to find people everywhere. 'This is unreal,' I thought. I was overcome by shyness. 'Who are they? What are they all doing here?' I asked Nicola.

'Extras, prop people, set painters, camera people, sound people, runners...' she said. The list was endless. It was a total contrast to the shoot for 'A Moment Like This', which was a simple performance filmed in double quick time and later cut with a montage of *X Factor* clips. When I filmed 'A Moment Like This', no one knew who was going to win the show, so the three finalists each made a video of the same song on the same day in a West End theatre. I remember singing the song through a few times, wearing a lovely black dress, and that was it. I didn't realise how complex the process could actually be.

For 'Bleeding Love' I was on set for six hours wearing a ridiculously expensive Dolce&Gabbana crystal-encrusted dress that weighed a tonne (well, eighteen kilograms, to be accurate). It cost tens of thousands of pounds, so I had to be very careful not to damage it. Needless to say, the stylist was hovering around me, on edge, for most of the day!

At the start of the shoot, I felt quite nervous and unsure of what I was doing. It was difficult having loads of people around while I was trying to emote into a camera, especially as I was relatively inexperienced. Melina gave me a lot of helpful direction: 'OK, the man you love has just left you and you're feeling really emotional,' she'd say. 'Now walk along the hallway looking into the camera.'

She patiently demonstrated different movements and positions to hold, but I still found the whole thing very nerve wracking until she cleared the set of everybody apart from the people who absolutely had to be there. It was only then that I started to feel comfortable.

I put lots of personal touches into the video: I decorated my 'bedroom' in turquoise and pinks, colours that I love, and hung a birdcage up in the apartment. I've loved birdcages ever since I saw a massive cage filled with flowers when I was on holiday in the Caribbean. The cage door was always open and there were birds flying around it and in and out of it. I thought it was really beautiful the way the birds came and went as they pleased; they still had their freedom, but there was somewhere to shelter if they needed it. Ever since then, I've had birdcages in my house and I often put flowers in them. I don't keep birds, though. I like the symbolism of having a cage with no bird in it; for me, it's a symbol of freedom and love.

All in all, shooting the 'Bleeding Love' video turned out to be a great experience and I was very happy with the end result. However, the word from my record company in America was that it wouldn't connect with their audience. They wanted me to film another video that was more 'American' with more of a storyline and an American backdrop. I was surprised, because I didn't know at the time that the American market was so markedly different to Europe. But I didn't mind: I was excited about making another video, especially as we decided to shoot it in New York, which is one of my favourite cities in the world.

We shot the alternative version in New York with a great director called Jesse Terrero. It was a very hard shoot, because we filmed in the freezing cold all day and half the night in the middle of Times Square: I had self-heating patches stuck all over my body under my clothes! To make it worse, there were even more people on this shoot than there were on the first one. Runners kept coming up and saying, 'Are you all right? Do you need anything?' I found it very weird to have people rushing around after me. That's not my thing at all. Still, it was worth it in the end, because it was a great-looking video and my record company loved it.

I had no idea what would happen when 'Bleeding Love' was released. Would people like it? Would they love it as much as I did? I hoped that they would connect with what I was doing, but what if they didn't feel it? I was totally on edge as the big day got closer. It was a really exciting time.

'Bleeding Love' was released on 22 October 2007 and I was totally shocked when it went straight to Number One in the UK, where it stayed for seven weeks. It also debuted at Number One in the Irish Singles Chart and went on to do really well all around Europe, in New Zealand and Australia. I was amazed, just over the moon! It felt so wonderful to be getting my music out there and to know that people were connecting with it.

Things had been relatively quiet for me up until I started promoting 'Bleeding Love', but then the whirlwind began again. All of a sudden I started flying here, there and everywhere, performing, doing interviews and shoots. There was no time for a day off. In fact, I was lucky if I had an hour off! But I wasn't complaining. As long as I was getting to do my music, I was happy.

At the end of October, I was invited to perform for the Live Lounge section of the Jo Whiley Show on Radio 1, singing one of my songs and a song by another artist. I sang 'Bleeding Love' and a cover of 'Run', a song by Snow Patrol, backed by a fourteen-piece band. To my amazement, the next day my version of 'Run' was requested thousands of times on the Chris Moyles Show. It was even added to the Radio 1 A playlist. I was amazed that it was so popular and it made me half-wish that I had recorded it for my album.

Life was a mad round of promotion for the next couple of months, with a quick break for Christmas at home with my family. The year ended on a real high for me. Not only had 'Bleeding Love' sold a million copies, making it the bestselling single of 2007, but my album, *Spirit*, had become the UK's fastest selling debut album of all time. I just could not believe that it had been received so well. Every time someone from the record company rang to tell me the latest figures, I felt dizzy with happiness. It was a dream come true and I felt so grateful to all the people who had supported me and my music and bought the record. I was also incredibly thankful to my friends and family for being there and supporting me all the way through. Everyone was happy for me. It was a really joyful time.

In January 2008, I was invited to sing at the Brit Awards ceremony and nominated for four awards. I was so, so thrilled. I thought back six years to when I was a Brit School student in the Brits audience, wishing so hard that I could get up on stage and sing. Now my dream was coming true. I was actually going to perform there!

I didn't expect to win an award, although obviously I hoped I would. It was enough just to be a part of it. Sitting at my table after I'd performed 'Bleeding Love', I heard cheering from one section of the audience. I looked over to see all the students from my old school. 'Brit student!' they were shouting.

'Yeah!' I shouted back.

'Well done! We love you!'

I was already on a high from performing, but suddenly I felt an even bigger rush of happiness. Wow, I thought, that used to be me! I can't actually believe that I'm sitting at the tables with artists that I used to look at admiringly when I was in the audience.

A lot of people seemed to expect me to be upset not to win an award. The thing is, I feel like I was recognised because I was nominated, and not winning is also part of the whole awards thing. It happens. You can't have everything, especially when you're just starting out. I would have loved to win a Brit and it really would have been a huge honour, but there's always next time. Honestly, I was just grateful to be there. The most important thing to me is to keep singing and creating and for people to keep enjoying what I'm doing. That's it, really. Not winning an award just spurred me on and gave me something else to look forward to in the future. So let's see what happens.

It's been suggested that maybe there was a bit of snobbery at work that night and perhaps I didn't win anything because I came up through a reality show. That's fair enough, I guess. Some people might not know that I've done the same circuit as every other artist who has been signed. Either way, I believe that I would still have managed to get to where I am if I hadn't gone on *The X Factor*, because I am positive that people can still do it that way, even though the industry has changed and it's a lot harder these days. You can make it if you stay dedicated and don't give up, definitely. But I just went a different route.

In America they don't have that 'reality show' preconception of me and I'm like every other artist who has been signed. It's different there, anyway. The US audience embraces *American Idol* winners like Kelly Clarkson and Carrie Underwood. But in the UK, so many people in and out of the industry have said, almost begrudgingly: 'I don't ever listen to *X Factor* artists, but I bought your album and I really love it.' So I've won some people over!

The Brits soon paled into insignificance for me, because of what came next. The following day, I got on a plane to South Africa with my dad, my boyfriend Lou and a representative from Sport Relief, little knowing that this trip would change my life view forever.

Just before the Brits, I had been into the studio to record the official Sport Relief single, 'Footprints In The Sand', which would be released the following month as a double-A side with 'Better In Time'. Now I was going to Johannesburg to see how some of the money raised in 2007 had been spent on various projects around the city. I knew that it was going to be an emotional time, as I had attended several lectures and discussions about the problems in South Africa. But I was still looking forward to it. I had no idea how much it would affect me.

The first day I visited Leth'ithemba Care Centre for children affected by HIV/AIDS in a township about half an hour outside Johannesburg. Most of the children there had lost one or both parents, so it just about broke my heart to meet them. And yet, as I wrote in my diary of the visit, 'I was met by a sea of beaming faces of children dancing and singing to us. Seeing their joy but knowing the sadness and tragedy they face was overwhelming.'

I was shocked by the living conditions in the township. It was far worse than I had imagined. None of the houses had any windows and there was murky water leaking from open drainpipes everywhere. I stayed and played with the children, who taught me some African nursery rhymes. One of the rhymes was about the dangers of AIDS. It was an awareness-raising song, but it made me sad to hear children singing about something so serious and dark.

That afternoon, I was invited to one of the children's homes. 'I took a package of food and gave it to their grandmother,' I wrote in my diary. 'It contained a bit of rice and a small amount of meat. Barely enough for one, never mind this family of five.

'Gran welcomed me into the tiny house like I was one of the family. It had three rooms, no inside toilet or anywhere to wash. It was total poverty. The brothers and sisters had lost their mum to AIDS a year before and were being looked after by their gran. I started to cry as she told me about the family's day-to-day struggle. Tears rolled down her cheeks too. There was something utterly devastating about an old lady breaking down like that.

'She told me how she desperately missed her daughter. The death has torn the family apart. And gran told me they sometimes go for days without food. She held my hand and said: "If it wasn't for the centre, we wouldn't eat today."

'The children's grandmother was maybe as old as eighty. Her great worry was over what would happen to the children when she passed away. Who would look after them? They wouldn't be able to run the house on their own.'

I couldn't stop crying; I will never, ever forget that day as long as I live. I realised that if it weren't for the fundraising of Sport Relief, many families would not survive.

The next day I went to a community radio station in Tembise township that money from Sport Relief helps to fund. The station is instrumental in putting out sexual health messages and it also has a centre where disadvantaged children can learn journalism skills. That afternoon I visited a settlement of nine hundred people where there is no running water and many of the inhabitants suffer from disease, dehydration and depression. 'I felt ill with sadness,' I wrote. These people were living in unimaginably bad conditions. I felt awful going back to my hotel, where there was an abundance of food and water.

Finally, on my third day, we went to watch a very athletic, competitive girls' football match, which had been organised as part of a team programme called Happy Hearts. I knew that the children and young adults in the programme were from households suffering from domestic violence, but I was stunned when I heard that many of the girls had been raped. It was devastating to think about the traumas they had been through.

'I've only been here a short time but it has been a life-changing experience,' I wrote at the end of the trip. 'Seeing what these brave, humble, remarkable people have to endure on a daily basis has put a lot of things in perspective for me. We have everything. They have nothing.'

I had only skimmed the surface of Johannesburg's troubles, but on my way back from South Africa, I decided that it was time to get more involved in charity work. I was determined to help as much as I could. Already, the proceeds from 'Footprints In The Sand' were going to Sport Relief when it was released in early March. I also auctioned off the blue Roberto Cavalli dress that I had worn while performing 'Bleeding Love' at the Brits. As well as Sports Relief, I've worked with Action for Children (NCH), World Society for the Protection of Animals, (WSPA), Make A Wish, Rays of Sunshine, Nelson Mandela's charity 46664, the Prince's Trust and lots more. I'm striving to be a part of as many others as I can. I get so many requests now and I feel so blessed to be in a position to help, so I'll continue to do all I can for as many as I can.

The pace of life kept getting faster. Just after Sport Relief, I had a call from my management company saying that I had been invited onto *The Oprah Winfrey Show*. I literally screamed at this news. My whole family has been watching Oprah since I was a baby, so I grew up with her, and I couldn't believe that I was getting the chance to appear on such a massive American TV show. Oprah was actually going to allow me to come on and sing! It was a huge thing. My single had been released in America and had broken into the Billboard Hot 100, but this could make a real difference to how many people heard my music.

I flew to Chicago a couple of days before the show. I wanted to make sure that my voice had time to recover from the journey and sometimes the air conditioning on airplanes gives me a sore throat, because it's very drying. So I was prepared vocally, but everything had happened so quickly that I didn't have time to figure out what to wear on the show. Instead, a stylist put a few bags of clothes together for me and I took them with me.

I spent the next two days in a complete panic trying on different outfits. After mixing up all the various looks the stylist had suggested, I must have tried on a hundred combinations. On the morning of the show, I still didn't know for sure what I was going to wear. I had narrowed it down to three dresses and picked out a lot of jewellery, but the whole thing was so scary that I just couldn't make my mind up. In the end, after all that, I went for a simple black dress and black shoes!

As I arrived at Harpo Studios in Chicago, where Oprah is filmed, I saw that the walls were lined with photos of Oprah and her guests over the years. It was overwhelming to see, and awesome to

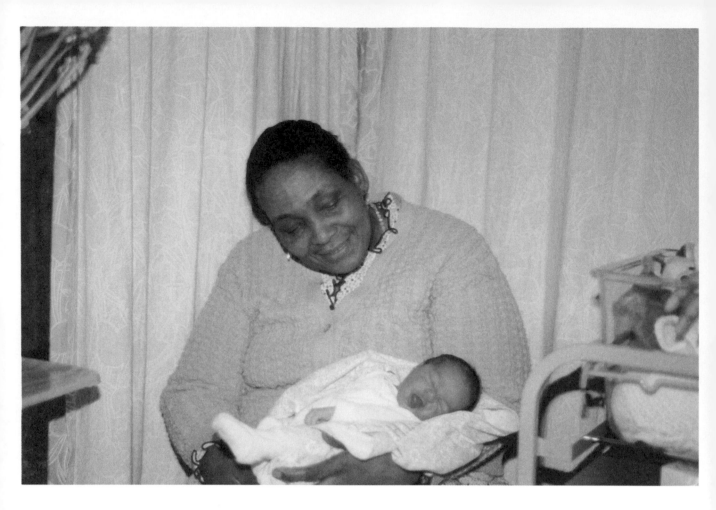

With my Grandmother and my Mother

Following pages:
With my Grandfather
School days

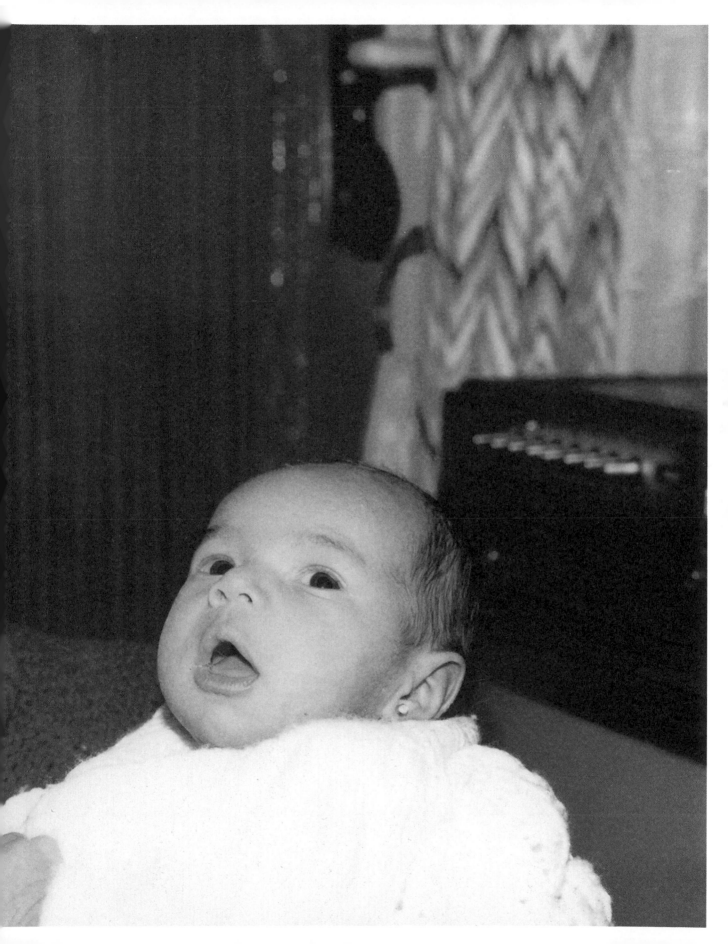

think of the difference that *The Oprah Winfrey Show* can make to someone's career. I felt like all my dreams had come true just being there. It was such a big moment.

I got a really nice vibe from Oprah when I met her. I think she's just amazing and I admire her so much for all that she does, including her charity work. She's very blessed, but she has tried to help other people and make a difference to their lives, and that's all you can do.

First I sang 'Bleeding Love' and then I sat down and had a little chat with Simon Cowell and Oprah. 'Wow!' Oprah kept saying. 'Talk about a star is born. You're the real deal, girl.'

How amazing is that? I was on such a high when I went back to my dressing room. 'We did it!' I said to Nicola. 'Can you believe it?'

'*Oprah*!' she burst out. 'Oprah!' Then she started crying. So I started crying. Then Ben, who does my hair, came in, took one look at us and said, 'Oh no, you're going to set me off!' So he started crying (and he never cries!) Jane, the make-up lady, went off to find us all a tissue, but when she came back, she was crying as well. We were all, 'Owoooahooo!' It was really funny!

Then Dad arrived. He just stood there laughing at us. 'What the hell is going on?' he said.

'It's just so emotional!' we said, and we all ended up in a group hug.

Jamie Oliver was there that day and so he popped into the dressing room next to say hello and say how proud he was. Then Simon came in, too. So it was 'a big old UK love-off', as Nicola later called it. I'm not always a very good judge of character, but there are certain people that you simply know are good, and Nicola is one of them. She's not just someone I work with; she's a dear friend whom I can talk to about anything and confide in. I'm so glad that I've met her.

When the show was over, Simon and I walked out of the studios together, followed by a documentary crew who were making a behind-the-scenes film. Just at that precise moment, a massive tour bus full of sightseers came past. We could hear the tour guide saying, 'And this is Oprah Winfrey's studio…'

All at once, the people in the coach turned their heads and looked straight at Simon. Instantly they started banging on the windows. 'It's Simon Cowell! It's Simon Cowell!'

One of the things I love about Simon is best demonstrated by what he did next: he strolled across the road, got on the tour bus, grabbed the mic off the tour guide and said, 'Hi, everyone, how are you?' They all went absolutely crazy!

I thought, 'Who does that?' I can't imagine myself doing it. Never! But Simon was loving the attention – and I think that's why people really love him, because he's got a great sense of humour, he's so into what he does and he's honest about it. I actually think he adores the fame. That's good because it comes with success and you should enjoy it if you can.

Simon's a natural when it comes to all of that, whereas it was a little bit harder for me to adjust. In the beginning I felt pressurised, nervous and a bit scared by all the attention I was getting. I've learned to enjoy myself a bit more now, though some aspects of it are still quite hard to get used to. When I'm on the red carpet and fifty people with cameras are shouting at me at the top of their voices, I sometimes think, 'Whoah!' I'm still me when I go out there, but I have to block it out a little bit, even if I'm more comfortable with it now than I used to be.

About ten days after I was on *The Oprah Winfrey Show*, Nicola called me into her hotel room and told me to sit down. 'What is it? What's wrong?' I said, my heart thumping.

'Nothing's wrong,' she said, grinning. 'You're number one in America!'

I was totally shocked. 'I've got to tell my family!' I yelled. I got straight on the phone to share it with them. 'Mum, you're never going to believe this…!'

That night we decided to celebrate by going to a Thai restaurant and then on to a club. As we were about to go out, Nicola beckoned me into her room, 'Just come in here for a moment, will you?'

A deafening explosion of party poppers resounded in my ears as I walked through the door, where there was a crowd of cheering people. The bangs were so noisy that they sounded like guns firing and they made everyone jump and start. Glitter went everywhere. Huge helium balloons bounced around the room and streamers fell on our heads. It was happy, crazy chaos in Nicola's room! I hate to think what the guests in the adjoining rooms thought we were doing in there.

When things had calmed down a bit, we all went to dinner. After the main course, the waiters brought in a big chocolate cake that said 'Congratulations!' on it. Afterwards, we went to a club called Les Deux and partied away until the morning. Two of my songwriting friends came along to join us: Claude Kelly, who wrote 'Forgive Me' with me, and Novel, who wrote 'Whatever It Takes'. It was a really good fun night.

A couple of days later I flew to New York to do promotion for my album. My best friend Aysha flew out with my cousin Yasmin; my brother came as well, and Mum and Dad were already with me, so on my 23rd birthday in early April, about twenty of us went out to Lucky Cheng's Downtown Drag Cabaret Dinner Theatre. It's a brilliant place. You eat your food while all these drag queens sing karaoke. At one point, a drag queen pulled a man up from his table, sat him on a raised chair and danced for him, doing all these crazy movements. Next there was a competition with a prize of a bottle of champagne for the best girl dancer who dared to go up and dance with the poor guy who had been in the chair. So of course my crazy friend Aysha got up to dance and she ended up spanking him, which won her the bottle of champagne!

The next day I went to see *The Little Mermaid* at the theatre, which I loved. Broadway is an awesome place, so buzzing and full of life. Seeing the show brought back to me just how much I have always adored musicals and reminded me of when I appeared in *Carousel* as a child. It got me thinking. Perhaps I could include my love of musicals in my work, somehow?

Those few days in New York were very special for me. Now that I had launched my career in America, life was so busy that there was a lot less time to see my friends and family. There were so many positives in my life that I couldn't complain, but I really, really missed them. It meant a lot to be able to hang out with the people I love most and have some fun.

SPOTLIGHT

To go from no one knowing me to everyone knowing me was very strange. The moment I appeared on TV, people in the street started saying, 'Look, it's Leona from *The X Factor*!' It happened overnight, which was crazy. So many strangers seemed to know my name, but back then it was only ever my first name. People never called me Leona Lewis. It was always: 'Hi, Leona, can I get your autograph?' or 'Can I get a picture, Leona?' They were very upfront about coming up to talk to me. I was Leona, the girl next door, plucked out of obscurity.

That changed after I had made my album. Then everyone started saying, 'Look, it's Leona Lewis!' It was funny how that happened. All of a sudden I acquired a surname. It wasn't exactly a mark of respect, but maybe it was an acknowledgement that I had grown up and become a professional artist. Now I've been nominated for the Grammys and the Brits, I think people see me in a different light, especially younger people. Strangers have stopped rushing up to me to ask me to sign things, or at least fewer people come up these days. Instead I hear voices whispering, 'Hey, that's Leona Lewis!'

It's kind of weird hearing my name being whispered. A few months ago, I took my little nephew, Brandon, to a city farm. As we wandered around looking at the animals, people were getting their camera phones out and taking pictures; I could hear them murmuring my name and they were staring, too. I'm more prepared for that sort of thing when I'm on the road and doing shows, but it doesn't feel the same when I'm doing ordinary day-to-day things.

It's almost as if people don't expect me to be a normal person who goes to the city farm and feeds the sheep. 'Oh my God, is that Leona Lewis?' they say, shocked. They seem to think I should be somewhere else doing something else. 'What are you doing here? Didn't I read that you were rehearsing in a studio in America?' Sometimes it can be quite funny and people are usually sweet and nice with it, but it can also be a little strange.

I'm lucky, because I have a circle of really close friends. I would call all of my friends best friends, because I don't really hang out with people who are just acquaintances that I see every now and again. Still, no one totally understands quite what fame is like unless they're also living it, so it helps to have a friend or two who is also in the public eye.

Keisha Buchanan from the Sugababes is a good friend. She was the first person I got to know who is well known by the public, and she understands what it's like. She's a great girl and we share the same values and morals, so we get on really well. And when we go out, people don't just stare at me: they're whispering about Keisha as well! It takes the pressure off a bit.

Meeting Keisha really helped me, because I could talk to her about some of the issues that come with fame and she could relate to the things I was experiencing, like people pretending to be your friends but not really being your friends. Since *The X Factor*, a lot of people have come out of the woodwork saying, 'Hey, do you remember me?' and wanting to meet up. That's nice if it's genuine, but there has been the occasional person along the way who was not being genuine, and it took me a while to figure that out. Actually, I still am figuring it out, but I'm much better at knowing the real people from the fake people now. I realise that this sort of thing happens to everyone in life and not just if you become famous. If people think that you can help them to get somewhere, there are those who will cling on to you to get something for themselves. So you have to be careful.

It's always nice to bump into the Sugababes when I'm working; we often meet backstage at different events. Like me, they were invited to play at Nelson Mandela's ninetieth birthday concert in Hyde Park in June, 2008. Annie Lennox and Josh Groban were among the other performers.

The concert was held to celebrate the former South African president's big day and raise funds for his HIV/AIDS charity 46664, so-called because he was 'Prisoner 46664' for twenty-seven years before his release from jail in 1990. As I've said, I'm now a 46664 ambassador for the Nelson Mandela Foundation, so I was very keen to be there and help out. It was the first big outdoor concert I had played and it was just amazing to be a part of it.

I grew up hearing about Nelson Mandela from my auntie Laurette, who absolutely loves and adores him. Nelson Mandela has always been a huge inspiration to her. She has pictures of him in her house and she used to teach me songs about him fighting for freedom in Africa. In fact, my auntie taught me everything I know about Nelson Mandela.

Auntie Laurette has always been there for me and supported my music, so she was the obvious person to take along with me to Mandela's ninetieth birthday dinner in Hyde Park the night before the concert. It was the first big event that she had been to with me and she was really thrilled.

First there was a drinks reception in a small marquee. It was full of famous faces. At one point, I was standing in the corner watching Will Smith schmoozing around with loads of people, and all I could think was: 'Oh my God, it's Will Smith!'

Just then, my auntie went up to him and said, 'You have to come here and take a picture with my niece Leona!' She dragged him over to me and then she took a photo of us. It was the most embarrassing thing that's ever happened to me in my life! He didn't mind. He was laughing. 'Your auntie is so funny!' he said. 'She's told me all about you.'

'Oh my god!' I said to her later. 'I can't believe you made Will Smith come over for a picture.'

Before we went into the dinner, we were told that no one was allowed to ask anyone for autographs or photos. We were taken from the small tent into a huge tent decorated with animal prints and masks and lots of brightly coloured flowers. A steel band was playing as we walked through the entrance and a huge African choir began to sing. It was incredible!

Forest Whitaker was there, as well as Jada Pinkett Smith, Oprah Winfrey, Lewis Hamilton, Naomi Campbell, the Sugababes, Robert de Niro and Denzel Washington. Will Smith hosted. Bill Clinton gave a speech, and so did Forest Whitaker. Gordon Ramsay did the cooking.

And guess what? My auntie went up to every single person in that tent and got their autograph. 'You're not allowed to do that!' I said.

'They didn't mind; they were fine!' she laughed.

When Nelson Mandela came into the room, she started crying. It was really emotional for her. She couldn't believe that she was actually in the same room with him. I was so happy that I had been able to make it possible.

Forest Whitaker gave an amazing speech. He is one of my favourite actors, so it was awe-inspiring to meet him. We had to hide from Will Smith, though, because he kept going round the tables taking the mickey out of people. I kept my head down, hoping against hope that he wouldn't come over and embarrass me.

At one point I went over said hi to Oprah and had a chat. She's so giving and always has time for you, so it was really nice to see her again. Then Elton John came over to our table and hung out for a little bit. He told me he was a big fan of my singing, which really put a smile on my face.

A little later, I took a leaf out my auntie's book, plucked up all my courage and made a beeline for Denzel Washington. 'Excuse me, sorry,' I said to the guy standing next to him. 'Can I just ask Denzel something?' I turned to Denzel and asked, 'Would you mind having your photo taken with me? I'm a huge, huge fan.' The guy with him said, obligingly, 'Sure, go ahead, I'll just wait over here.'

After we took the photo, Auntie Laurette sidled up and said, 'Why on earth did you just elbow Robert de Niro out of the way?'

'What?' I said, shocked. 'What are you talking about?'

'You asked Robert de Niro to step aside so you could have your photo taken with Denzel Washington!'

I turned round. It *was* Robert de Niro standing there! I hadn't noticed him because I was so focused on Denzel! Also, it was before I'd had laser eye surgery for my bad eyesight. I was completely mortified, as you can imagine, because I think Robert de Niro is a wonderful actor. It was so embarrassing. I sheepishly went back to our table.

After dinner, there was an auction to raise money for the Nelson Mandela Foundation. Naomi Campbell was bidding for a necklace that went for something like a million pounds, I think. It was craziness. Obviously I didn't try and get anything. It was well out of my league.

The following morning I did a photo call with Nelson at the Intercontinental Hotel in Hyde Park, along with all the other people who were taking part in the concert that day. Afterwards, we all had individual photos taken with him, which was absolutely amazing, especially as we held hands. I felt so honoured. He's so lovely and sweet and he emanates peacefulness and calm. I gave him a letter from the children at my auntie's charity, which he happily accepted.

All my family was at the concert to see me sing 'Bleeding Love' and 'Better In Time', so it was a very emotional event, all told. I was really nervous because I hadn't performed in front of such a big London crowd before, but it went really well.

I was near to Nelson just as he was about to go on stage. He was in his chair and his people were saying, 'No, you can't walk out there! You need to stay seated.' But despite being old and frail, he got up out of the chair and walked onto the stage to greet the cheering crowd. I was so moved. The audience went absolutely crazy. 'Even as we celebrate, let us remind ourselves that our work is far from complete,' he said. 'Where there is poverty and sickness, including AIDS, where human beings are being oppressed, there is more work to be done. Our work is for freedom for all.'

'How is he doing this, at ninety years old?' I thought. He's having so many birthday celebrations around the world, and yet he keeps on going. He's a very strong person. I found him totally inspiring.

Life doesn't get any better than when you meet one of the world's most loved and admired iconic figures and get to sing at his birthday party. However, the summer of 2008 had another massive highlight in store for me.

I was completely incredulous when I was asked to represent London in Beijing at the closing ceremony of the 2008 Olympics, in preparation for the handover of the Olympic torch to London

2012. I felt so, so honoured to be involved. It was especially important to me, because a lot of the 2012 Olympic money is going towards funding regeneration in Hackney and east London.

As I've said, I'm proud of where I grew up and where I come from, so I'm keen to help improve the area. I really want London – and Hackney – to be a better place in which to live and work. Both the area where I live and the local community have a lot of potential for opportunity and growth, which is why the funding is so vital. People worry that regeneration could lead to people being forced out of the area by high costs and property hikes, but hopefully that won't be the case and they will be able to take advantage of the increased funding instead.

Hackney needs more job opportunities, better schools and colleges. Money is desperately needed to improve the living environment and provide more sports and outdoor activities, especially for younger people. It's a troubled area and there's a lot of crime.

One of the problems is that many youths in Hackney don't have anything to do, so they're bored and as a result they're off committing crimes. Boredom combined with poverty and lack of education inevitably leads to social breakdown. We need more investment in the area; we need more police too. I'm hoping that London 2012 will make a big difference.

There is a shocking contrast between Hackney and wealthier areas of London, like Knightsbridge and Chelsea. You see the differences, even in the advertising. In Hackney, the billboards are all about pawnbrokers, fizzy drinks, alcohol and fast food. You see far less of that kind of thing in the rich boroughs. It really makes me upset.

The number of young boys who have died from knife and gun crime in Hackney is shocking. It has to stop. I know people who have been affected by knife and gun crime and I think it's just so sad. It's a total waste of life. I used to worry a lot about my younger brother Kyle walking around in streets where people are carrying knives and guns. Maybe they're just carrying them to protect themselves, but at the end of the day, if you've got a weapon, you may use it. Fortunately, now that Kyle is older, I'm not as worried as I used to be.

How can we combat such problems? Well, there are already some great music projects in the borough, which work really well, because there are a lot of young people in Hackney who are very musically inclined. There are some good youth organisations as well, and the Hackney Empire has some excellent initiatives going on. But we need a lot more.

Sometimes it seems that people looking in from the outside have a different perception of what will and won't work from those of us who live in Hackney. I come from a huge family. My father is one of eleven brothers and sisters, so I've got lots of young cousins and nephews throughout the area. I know what they are thinking and the challenges they are facing, so I think I have some insight into what needs to be done.

Some of the community projects that are introduced end up not working because they are devised from an outsider's perspective. It doesn't make sense to me when they shut down the community centres and try to focus kids on discussion events on estates, because kids don't really want to get involved in discussions and talks, they want to do things! It seems to me that you can easily incorporate discussions into activities, anyway. These things really need to be addressed with younger people's perspectives in mind, I think. On the other hand, the community also has to want to make things better. A lot of people say, 'No, we don't need help,' but they have to be willing to participate if things are going to change. I can help out now, but when I've done my thing and I have a bit more experience, I'd definitely like to help more. That's why I jumped at the chance to get involved in the summer Olympics 2008 closing ceremony. And when they told me that I would be performing with Jimmy Page from Led Zeppelin, well that was the icing on the cake! He's just incredible, a total legend.

It was so cool to be singing a Led Zeppelin song. Although I hadn't grown up with their music, I obviously knew who they were and I loved their songs, especially 'Stairway To Heaven,' everyone's favourite. I wasn't there the first time around when 'Whole Lotta Love' was released, but I knew the guitar riff well from *Top Of The Pops*. I always associated it with the chart countdown, which I watched avidly all through my childhood, so it was weirdly familiar when I came to record the song.

I went to meet Jimmy in a rehearsal studio in Mile End, London, just to say hello, initially. He's one of the nicest people I've ever met. He's just really, really sweet. He had to agree the version I was going to do, which was quite nerve wracking, because it's a big song and it's his song and I really wanted him to like my version. Luckily, he was very enthusiastic when he heard it. I recorded it with the producer Steve Robson, and managed to lay down most of the vocals in a day. I was in the kitchen making tea at the studios when Jimmy walked in and gave me a hug. 'Thank you, it's amazing! I'm blown away,' he said. 'I love what you've done with it.'

So now we had the song, it was time to focus on the performance. The plan was for the Olympic flag to be handed to the Mayor of London, Boris Johnson. Then there would be an eight-minute presentation to celebrate the upcoming 2012 Olympics, with a London-themed performance involving a red double-decker bus, bicycles and people dressed as commuters.

Jimmy and I would appear from inside the bus, which was specially adapted to open up like a lotus flower, and I would rise up on a platform to a height of about ten metres and sing, while Jimmy played guitar on a lower level. David Beckham was also a part of the presentation; he was going to emerge from the bus at the end of 'Whole Lotta Love' and kick a football into the crowd.

I rehearsed in a warehouse in Mile End. At the first rehearsal, I rose up on a hydraulic platform, like the ones window cleaners use to work on big buildings. I just went a little way, to get used to the idea. For the second rehearsal, I experimented with rising up out of the bus, but the pole couldn't be raised to the full height because the ceiling wasn't high enough and I would have gone through the roof.

At the final rehearsal, we took the bus outside and I tested going even higher. It was quite daunting! Way below, my mum looked up at me, aghast. She suffers from vertigo and doesn't even like climbing ladders, so she found it hard to imagine how I could go so high without freaking out.

Sadly, my dog Suzie died during this time. I was so upset that I had to miss a couple of rehearsals. I couldn't even bear to leave the house. We'd had Suzie since she was six weeks old and she was seventeen when she died, so I barely remember life before her. It was so weird not having her around. She had been my little best friend ever since I was six. She was a Yorkshire Terrier and absolutely tiny. All of my dolls' clothes fit her, so I was always dressing her up in dolly dresses; I put little hats on her, made her little legwarmers and kitted her out in tiny Santa outfits and Easter outfits. My friend also had a Yorkie and we dressed them both up and married them in the park one day, so she had a little husband too. Oh, the poor thing! Fortunately, as I grew older, I started treating her like a proper dog, which she was probably very happy about.

When I moved out of home during *The X Factor*, we decided that it wasn't fair to uproot Suzie and take her to a new place, so she stayed with my mum and they kept each other company. So Mum was distraught when she passed away. It was almost as if she'd lost a child; it was that painful for her. We love animals so much, my mum and me, and they really do become part of your family. But, as my dad says, Suzie had such a good life and she lived a very, very long time, so that's what you have to focus on.

I felt bad for missing rehearsals, but the production team were all very understanding and it wasn't long before I was back on the elevating platform, trying to get used to singing at a great height. Then they put the bus in a container and shipped it over to China, where it arrived three weeks later.

Being in Beijing felt quite surreal. It's so different, so busy, and there are so many people there. It's modern and clean, but it also has a lot of traditional architecture. So there's this high-tech modern downtown area that contrasts wonderfully with its beautiful, ancient ornamental gardens.

I was there with Mum and Dad and Lou for ten days and we saw quite a bit of the city and surrounding area. We even saw the Great Wall, which was amazing. Another highlight was visiting an amazing silk market, which was a bit like Hackney market, except that it was on five floors in a building in the middle of China, with crazy market people chasing you around. You have to haggle people down when you buy something; I wasn't very good at it, but Lou and Dad were.

My next set of major rehearsals took place at Camp Freddie, a disused airfield surrounded by forest, an hour and a half from Beijing, in the middle of nowhere. We arrived as night was falling, after a day of rehearsals with the dancers. I was nervous, because this was the first time that I was going to rise up to the full height out of the bus, which was in a massive aircraft hangar lit up by enormous floodlights. First I got inside the bus and was harnessed onto the pole. Then the mechanical lotus petals opened above me and I began to rise higher and higher, until I reached the full glaring beam of the massive floodlights above me.

Unfortunately, because it had just rained and we were so near the forest, the air was thick with big black bugs. They were attracted by the lights in their thousands, like moths to a gigantic flame. Even worse, each bug was the size of my fist! I have no idea what they actually were, but they looked like a cross between giant flying spiders and cockroaches. I have never seen anything like them in my life! (And I hope I never do again.)

There were thick nets under the lights: thousands upon thousands of bugs flew into the light, got zapped by the heat and fell dead into the nets. It was crazy and horrible. Way below me, a guy with a big white broom was sweeping them up into big piles. I'm telling you, they were everywhere. It was like the attack of the killer cockroaches. They were prehistoric looking and so heavy that they couldn't even fly straight. So it was impossible to predict which way they were going to go, which made it impossible to avoid them. They kept knocking into me as I went through the song, high on my tiny platform. Eurgh! It was disgusting. I tried to brush them off, but they were gluey and got stuck to my skin and tangled up in my hair. They were even flying into my mouth as I was singing. It was the most horrible thing I have ever, ever experienced.

Now, I love animals, but I am absolutely petrified of anything creepy-crawly. Flies, spiders, whatever – I have a real, real fear of them all. I would never kill anything, but I just don't like being around them. So this was my worst nightmare! When I finally came down, I was paralysed with fear. I couldn't speak or move. I was just horrified.

I pulled myself together after a couple of minutes. But the ordeal wasn't quite over. It was a five-minute walk across the airfield back into the main building and the floor was carpeted with millions of bugs. There were no lights attracting them now, but that also meant that you couldn't see where they were. Wearing flip flops, I hop-scotched my way back to the main building, virtually in tears. Luckily we only had to rehearse at Camp Freddie a few times. It was a big production with lots of machinery to move around, so they couldn't keep doing it. You can't imagine how relieved I was to get back to the city, away from those monster bugs.

Back in Beijing, I had a bit of a clothes crisis, because no one had told me that I would need to get dressed up for press calls, a photo call and the party after the closing ceremony. As a result, I didn't have any evening clothes with me at all – and it turned out that I really needed them. So I ran round the Beijing shopping centres for two days with Nicola and a translator who could barely speak English, trying desperately to find something suitable to wear.

We had the most ridiculous time in the Prada store. It was a promising start: I found a great-looking dress and went to the changing room to try it on. But when I came to take it off, I couldn't get the zip down, even though the dress was big on me. So there I was in the dressing room, with Nicola and a translator who couldn't understand a word we were saying, trying to unzip a dress that was worth thousands of pounds, without ripping it. Nicola kept saying, 'I just can't get the zip down!' but her pleas were being met with blank faces. Finally we collapsed into giggles because it was such an absurd situation.

In the end, I had to get the on-site tailor to come and help. So now I had the tailor and Nicola tugging away at this zip. By this point, I was starting to feel really hot and claustrophobic. Meanwhile Nicola was panicking because she thought we'd broken the dress and the tailor was telling us off. 'It's too tight!' he kept saying.

'No, it's not too tight!' we tried to explain. 'It's a bad zip.'

Then the sales assistant came in, so there were three people and the translator all huddled around me trying to undo this zip. Thankfully, it came undone eventually, which was a huge relief. We were so embarrassed after all the fuss that we just handed the dress back, saying we would come back later, and ran out of the shop as fast as we could. I was hoping that I would find another dress somewhere else, but despite the zip, the Prada dress turned out to be the one I wanted to wear. So the next day, I had to go back to the shop and shyly pick it up, hoping they had forgotten the fracas of the day before.

I wore the dress for my photo call with David Beckham. He was very sweet. 'I really like your music,' he said when we first met. 'Really proud of what you're doing. You've done so well. Congratulations.' We did a signing swap: I signed some stuff for his kids and he signed some stuff for my brothers!

Everyone was obsessed with him. Nicola reckoned he had the most manly walk you could ever see on a man. She kept taking pictures of him, but she was too embarrassed to take any from the front, so she ended up with a million pictures of the back of David Beckham.

The day of the show arrived with a blistering heat that just got hotter by the hour. A bus picked us up from our hotel to take us to Beijing's Bird's Nest Stadium. OK, we weren't expecting a showbiz bus, because we were in China, but this was a rickety old mini bus van with curtains in the windows.

Squashed up next to each other in this tiny van were: Lou, me, Mum, Dad, Nicola, Jimmy Page, Jimmy's mate and manager, David Beckham, David's friend, his PR person and the head of ceremonies for London Olympics 2012. Every time we pulled up at a traffic light, people on the pavement peeked in. Of course, the moment they saw David, they started screaming. Then, when we set off again, there would be a huge crowd chasing us down the road for miles, because it was such a broken up old van that it couldn't go very fast. It was bizarre.

Eventually we arrived at the first accreditation area for the stadium: there was an incredible amount of security in place. The bus had to go through loads of security checks and get swiped, while we got off and went through private security, individually. Then we got back on the bus and drove into the main arena. We pulled up next to this huge souped-up luxury coach. Lou looked out of the window and said, 'Look, there's Jackie Chan!'

'It's can't be,' someone said. 'It must be someone who looks like him.'

'No, it really is Jackie Chan!' said David.

We looked across at the luxury coach and there indeed was the one and only Jackie Chan, waving at us!

It was time to get ready for the biggest performance of my life. I couldn't help feeling nervous: not only would I be singing in front of a massive stadium crowd, but the TV audience for the ceremony was estimated to be in the *billions*. Plus, it was a phenomenally hot day, the kind of weather that makes you want to lie in an air-conditioned room drinking ice-cold water for hours on end.

We were taken to the bus underneath the stadium, where thousands of Chinese extras and dancers were rushing around. They all had directions to go here and there, and everyone followed them to a tee. I have no idea how the organisers managed to coordinate all those people. Somehow I don't think it would have worked so well in London! Everything was running so smoothly.

Jimmy, David and I waited for an hour before the bus actually pulled out into the stadium. There were all kinds of checks before we were strapped in and then everything was checked again. There was a lot going on, with people faffing around, getting on and off the bus, tying us in and making sure we were OK, tucking up all the bits and pieces. I couldn't move after I was harnessed in under my huge dress. There was no space even to hold a bottle of water. The heat was incredible; it was like being in a sauna times ten. I've never felt anything like it. Wearing my huge foil dress, I literally thought that I was going to pass out – and that's not even me exaggerating. I kept thinking, I'm going to faint; I'm going to faint right now!

Someone said, 'We have to close the doors now, Leona…' and suddenly the air was even hotter. I was paranoid about my hair going flat and my make-up running. I could imagine myself rising out of the bus like a drowned rat, with sweat pouring down my face. That would be a really good look! 'Please, don't let my make-up run!' I wailed. 'A billion people are going to be watching me.'

David was behind me, so I couldn't really see him, but Jimmy was next to me. 'Have a good one! Rock it!' he said.

I was praying that the petals of the bus would open, that the lights would come on, the pole would go up and that Jimmy and David would also rise up. So much could have gone wrong. I just wanted everything to go right.

The bus started and began to make its way slowly into the stadium. It crawled all the way around the arena at about five miles per hour and took forever to draw up in front of the officials' boxes. By now I was gasping and sweltering with heat. In fact, I don't know how the bus didn't blow up, because there was so much equipment on there and it was so, so hot. I was very worried about it. If the bus blew up, it would be a right show!

As the petals on the bus opened and I felt the soft flow of fresh air on my upturned face, I thought, 'Oh my God, yes!' In that moment I felt very grateful that I would be rising so high on the platform, because the higher I went, the cooler it would be. At last!

People were screaming as the bus opened and the performance began. With Jimmy on guitar beside me, I felt like a rock star. I wasn't thinking about how I was performing in front of one of the largest TV audiences in history, or that I may never have such wide exposure again in my life. I just got lost in the song and gave it everything I had. It was absolutely amazing and I loved every moment of it.

STAYING TRUE

I am very family and friends orientated, so it can be difficult being away from home so much. I get very homesick and I really miss the people who matter to me. Luckily, in these days of emails and texting, we can still stay in touch. I'm just a phone call away and my friends know that they can reach me if they need to. It is especially hard to be apart from my boyfriend, Lou, but we always make time for each other on ichat, text, mobile or Blackberry. That's the most important thing: even if you're not seeing each other the whole time, you just have to keep the communication going.

I've known Lou since I was ten and we got together when I was seventeen. He's such a great guy; he's very, very special. He's always been there for me, no matter what, right from the beginning, and he dedicates a lot of time to me. I'm very lucky to have him and his support; I also feel fortunate to have a boyfriend who is very honest with me. All the close people around me tell me what they think honestly and I really respect that.

Lou and I have wonderful holidays to make up for the time we spend apart. My idea of a romantic getaway would be to go skiing. I love the idea of coming back at the end of the day and warming up in front of a fire with a hot chocolate. Then again, I do love lounging on a beach all day as well. But I do most of my travelling for work, when it's not that relaxing!

My schedule is pretty hectic, but more and more I'm trying to see the places I'm visiting, rather than just flying in and out. I don't like going somewhere for two days and sitting inside a hotel room doing nothing but interviews. I want to connect with the people I'm bringing my music to, I want to get an insight into where they live and see the sights. So these days I try to go out a day early, so I can get a better sense of the place I'm visiting.

I really enjoyed visiting Japan. The people in Tokyo are lovely and the mix of modern technology and ancient tradition over there is just mind-boggling. It's like another world; it's so weird and so cool.

I felt as if I was living the life of a different person in Tokyo. The shopping there is insane. I loved just walking down the street and going into different gadget stores and seeing all the mad clothes in the shops. I tried on loads of different crazy things that I would never wear in a million years, just for fun. They've got some wild styles over there and they're not afraid to try something bold and different: it's a part of their lifestyle.

I get a lot of different influences from my travels. When I was in Japan, I saw some socks that had loads of satiny-lace ribbon around the top and I bought loads! They had shoe socks as well, which were really weird, but I bought some anyway. I haven't worn them yet, but I like having stuff from far off places in my wardrobe. You never know – I might find something to wear them with one day.

At one point, I had to buy pair of tights for a show I was doing. In Tokyo they have vending machines with tights in them, so I got some vending machine tights. They literally came up to my knees; I could not get them any higher than that. I was like, 'Are you serious?' After that, we had everyone searching for tights that would fit me. It was so funny.

One night we went to a traditional Japanese tofu restaurant where they bring you about ten different courses. Unfortunately, I got really sick about halfway through the meal. It was nothing to do with the food – I think it was a stomach bug – but it really upset the hosts that I had to leave. 'Oh my God, are you OK?' they kept saying. They really took it to heart.

'I'm just sick and I have to go,' I explained.

'What have we done?' they asked. 'My gosh, she's leaving!' one of them cried. It was all a bit of a drama, because being a good host is such a big thing in Japanese society. 'Oh dear,' I thought. 'I really hope I haven't offended anyone.'

I wanted to go out of Tokyo and see the countryside, but although there wasn't time, I hope to get the chance in the future. Fortunately, I was in Japan long enough to get quite a good sense of the place and know that I want to go back soon.

I love going to America, too. I'm spending more and more time in the States these days. I flew out there again in September 2008 to take part in a big televised concert for Stand Up To Cancer, a charitable campaign run by the Entertainment Industry Foundation. The overall project is aimed at raising funds for cancer research and I had been asked to join a group of female artists in singing 'Just Stand Up', the official single of the first campaign.

When my management company listed the other artists who would be involved in recording the single, I was totally shocked. Mariah Carey, Beyoncé, Ciara, Rihanna, Natasha Bedingfield, Fergie and Ashanti were just some of them! And the producers were Kenny 'Babyface' Edmonds and Antonio 'LA' Reid.

Not surprisingly, I was scared and nervous when I met everyone on the first day of rehearsals. We gathered in a massive studio in New York. There were mirrors across one wall and chairs across the other, so it felt a little like being in the first gym class of term. Nicola and I, typically British and very polite, sat in the corner, watching all these fierce girls come in. Everyone had their little entourage with them and they were all looking really fabulous. Rihanna was pushing a look; Beyoncé was pushing a look; and I was in a pair of fake Ugg boots, jeans and a top!

It was surreal seeing all these women in the same room together. We sat on the chairs and checked each other out in the mirror without saying anything at first. After a while we started chatting to the people next to us, and that slowly broke the ice.

The musical director called us all around the piano. 'Can everyone else leave the room?' he said. So the entourages went to wait outside, leaving the artists to get on with rehearsals. Things relaxed after that and we introduced ourselves properly. I had met Natasha Bedingfield before and it was nice to see her again. I had a good chat with Beyoncé, with Ciara and with Fergie, and I swapped numbers with Rihanna. She's so lovely, such a character.

It was quite daunting to be standing around the piano with a group of such amazing artists. Imagine being so close to your idols, people whose music you've listened to when you've been sad or happy and it's meant so much! It was amazing. 'Why am I here again?' I kept asking myself. It was very hard to believe it was happening. But then everyone started singing and I just went with it. It was great to be a part of it.

The single was released in late August and we all performed it in early September on the Stand Up To Cancer show, which aired simultaneously on three major American channels, ABC, CBS and NBC. It got to number eleven in the Billboard Hot 100, which was great.

Later in the month, I made a surprise appearance on stage with Lil' Wayne and T-Pain, at the 25th MTV Music Video Awards at Paramount studios. This really impressed my younger brother. He wasn't interested when I told him that I had sung with Mariah Carey, Rihanna and Beyoncé, or that I'd met Whitney Houston. But the moment I said I was singing with Lil' Wayne, he said, 'Oh my God, I can't believe it! What an honour.' It was a lot of fun, I must say.

But it had been a crazy few months of new projects and worldwide promotion, so by the time I came to fly back to England for a short break, I was feeling upset that I hadn't seen my friends in ages. Plus they were all saying, 'Hey, we really want to see you!' So, since I had a few days off, it seemed like the ideal time go away and do something girlie together, rather than coming home.

Three of my girlfriends and I decided to go to the Algarve in Portugal. We wanted to rent somewhere nice and secluded with a pool, because it's good to have some privacy.

Well, when we said *secluded*, we didn't mean in the middle of absolutely nowhere! 'Out of the way' just didn't describe it. There were no other houses for miles. There wasn't even a dirt road leading to our cottage and we had to get there across some fields in a four-by-four.

To make things harder, we arrived in the pitch-black dark. There were no lights to guide us, so it was crazy trying to find it. Luckily one of my friends had Sat Nav on her Blackberry. Otherwise, I don't know what we would have done. 'Why are we staying here again?' we kept asking as we made our bumpy way across the grass leading up to the front door.

The cottage was properly rural. We entered the hall and turned on the lights to see cobwebs hanging from the ceiling. 'Aaagh, spiders!' someone said. We jumped with fright, because we are all petrified of spiders. Huddling together, we made our way into the lounge, which was very pretty and rustic. But how many spiders were in there, hiding in the corners? We were all slightly on edge that first night.

Finally we went to bed. I was looking forward to a good long sleep after the journey and the excitement of earlier. But as I was snuggling up between the sheets, I saw a spider on the covers. Emitting a piercing shriek, I jumped out of bed and ran out of the room, calling for help. I know it's silly to be scared of spiders, because I know they can't hurt me, but they freak me out because they've got eight legs. Within seconds, all four of us were screaming and running around the house. When we had calmed down, we decided to sleep in one room together, for protection. But then my friend plucked up all her courage and somehow shooed the spider out of my bed, so I was able to sleep there again. She was so proud of herself.

It wasn't unusual to hear a loud scream from one of the bedrooms, but once we had settled in, we made the most of being together and had a great time. One night we made ourselves up as witches for a laugh; another night we dressed up in 1980s retro clothes and went off to a local restaurant, then on to a little club and a weird beach party.

I love having girls' nights in and hanging out with my mates: reading magazines; painting our nails; putting on face masks; listening to music; making tapes; and eating ice cream. Häagen Dazs Chocolate Chocolate Chip ice cream is my guiltiest pleasure. I feel sick every time I eat it – maybe I'm lactose intolerant, or something – but I just have to eat it anyway. I don't care if it makes me sick!

I'm crazy about film and there's nothing better than watching a great movie with your mates. I went round to my friend's recently because she was having a really hard time with her boyfriend; we watched *300* to cheer her up. It's full of muscle men. 'Is that body paint?' we kept saying, pointing at the screen and giggling. 'That can't be real, surely!'

After my holiday, we made the video for my fourth single, 'Forgive Me', which was produced by Akon. This time I was much more heavily involved in the creative process than I had been with my other videos, right down to the styling, the angles of the shots and even the edit.

A lot of my songs are ballads and very emotive, but 'Forgive Me' is different: it's uptempo, carefree and fun. I wanted a video that reflected that and revealed a different side to me than people had seen before.

The director Wayne Isham and I developed the idea together. We had a meeting at Lows hotel in Santa Monica and I told him how I'm crazy about theatre and musicals. 'I'd love to do something with that,' I said. He had originally come up with another idea, but we reworked it so that the video would incorporate references to a few different musicals, including *Singin' In The Rain*, *Carousel* and *West Side Story*.

It was a massive production. It took two days to film it on the New York street at Universal Studios, which was destroyed by fire a few weeks later, sadly. There were masses of dancers and extras. I was more used to having loads of people around on set by then and I really enjoyed singing and dancing through the different set ups. I didn't properly bust a move or anything. It wasn't about proper choreography, because I didn't want to do that. But there was a little bit of dance incorporated, so it was really fun.

By the time we filmed it, I felt a lot more confident in front of the camera. It always makes me laugh to think back to my first proper editorial photo shoot with *Harper's Bazaar*, where the photographer, Ralph Mecke, kept saying, 'Look into the camera. You need to emote and connect to the camera.'

I remember trying my hardest, doing all these poses – but about halfway through, he said, 'No, no, no! OK, Leona, I have to talk to you. We really need you to connect with the camera. We need your eyes to connect with the camera. We need people to look at you and see what I see when I'm looking at you in real life.'

He came up with a good suggestion: 'Picture someone's face and imagine that you're looking at their face,' he said. 'Connect whatever emotion you want to feel to the person whose face it is.

If you want to feel happy, think about someone who makes you feel happy. Who makes you sad or angry? Picture their face and imagine you're looking into their eyes when you're looking into the lens.'

I took on board what Ralph said when I did a shoot in a beautiful house in LA some time afterwards. The sun was bright and it was really summery and I thought of my gran, because I wanted to appear happy and reflective in the photographs. When I look back at them, there's just something really peaceful about them.

Now I often picture someone's face when I'm looking into the camera, because the photos seem to come out much better. I can really tell the difference between the ones where I'm picturing someone to the ones where I'm not.

My next video was for my fifth single, 'Run', a cover of a great song by Snow Patrol, a really amazing band. 'Run' is one of my favourite songs, musically, lyrically and melodically. It's so epic. As I said earlier, after I sang it for Live Lounge on Radio One, it became a frequent request. People kept telling me, 'We want a version of it. We want to get hold of it somehow.'

'Let's make the Live Lounge version available to everyone,' I suggested. But that wasn't possible, so I decided to try doing a studio version. I went into the studio and recorded it, but afterwards I remember thinking, 'It's not right. No, I'll have to do it again.'

'You can't do it again,' everyone said. 'We don't have time!'

'But I have to do it again, because there's something wrong,' I said.

I just couldn't feel the emotion of it. I don't know what the problem was; maybe I was feeling a bit blue the day I recorded it, or perhaps I was under pressure and just not connecting in some way. I needed to listen to it again, to delve deeply into the song. So I went away to America for a while, taking the music with me, and when I came back, I felt ready to go into the studio again.

'I want to record it on a hand-held mic, as if I'm singing onstage,' I said when I got to the studio. 'I'll record it a few times all the way through and that's all I'll do. I want to do it like it's one take.' And that's what I did.

'We got it!' I said afterwards. 'We've captured it!'

'OK, you were right,' my management company agreed. I was so happy.

It was a spur of the moment decision to make the video, so the turnaround period was just crazy. But that's all part of the fun. I don't know how we did it, though. It was a case of, 'OK, the pressure's on, let's get this going. Let's focus our attention.'

The video turned out a bit like a dream sequence. It starts on a dusty trail and moves into the forest and then to a cliff, so it's a really cool concept. Is she escaping? Is she hiding? Is she confronting something? Is she running away from something or running towards something? Is she going to jump off the cliff because she's running away from something? Or is she going to turn around, face her fears and battle all that's going on?

We flew to South Africa to shoot it in a forest, a timeless natural landscape that could be set in the past, present or future. I wanted my outfit to express a mismatch of time, so I envisaged wearing a Victorian-type dress with a massive skirt and corset, accessorised with heavy-duty chains, and my hair in a really modern style.

I wanted the dress to be specially made, but there wasn't enough time, really. Because of the quick turnaround, the poor dressmaker only had forty-eight hours to make it, which is ridiculous, so I don't know what I was expecting. It shouldn't have been a surprise that when it came back it just wasn't anything like I had imagined. I didn't think it was right, so we had to completely redo the whole thing: dye the fabric and start from scratch. We managed to get something together at the last minute, though. The dress was a bit ripped, so it hinted at the possibility that I had been running away from something or something had just happened to me.

After ten hours of styling, I went straight to the video set. The shoot took twenty-four hours. We started off in the sunlight and missed some of the shots, so we had to shoot the night scenes and then keep going through the next morning to capture the missed daylight scenes.

I didn't sleep all night. I had to stay fresh and awake and focused; I couldn't go in front of the camera with my eyes half closed. To keep from getting tired, I put on my iPod and danced around to uptempo songs by Rihanna and Jennifer Hudson - in my tiny Winnebago in the middle of the forest. 'I'm not tired! I'm not tired. All my energy's up!' I kept shouting.

Nicola was there and she helped keep me up. 'Come on, stay awake! It's all fun!' she said, again and again.

'Jane,' I asked the make-up lady when I started to droop, 'Can you paint eyeballs onto my eyelids, please?'

In the end, the desire to make a great video kept me going. It was only twenty-four hours of my life, after all, and it was a lot of fun, despite the pressure.

We finished at ten in the morning and we were due to fly home at around two o'clock in the afternoon. So there was just time to go to the hotel in Cape Town and spend an hour and a half there before we left for the airport. 'I feel all right,' I said to Nicola in the back of the Previa. 'In fact, I feel great! Maybe I'll go shopping.'

Nicola yawned as I chatted away. Suddenly, in mid-sentence, a huge wave of tiredness overtook me. My head dipped and I fell asleep, sitting up. Nicola nodded off too and we didn't stir until the driver woke us up when we got to the hotel, where I went straight to my room and got into bed. No shopping for me.

Usually I find it really easy to sleep on planes, but not when I'm doing a video, for some reason. Before and after video shoots, I get all wired and can't sleep. So on the way there and the way back, I just couldn't switch off, because the whole experience was so exciting and there were lots of thoughts buzzing around my brain.

We landed in London, immediately drove three hours to Liverpool for the MTV Europe Music Awards, and then drove three hours back to London. I got home at three in the morning. It was just crazily hectic.

So would I have had that week off if I hadn't made the 'Run' video? Of course not! One time I was supposed to have gone to Japan and Australia, but when that didn't happen, suddenly I had a million other things to do in England, from dress fittings to radio interviews. 'Wait a minute!' I said. 'I wasn't supposed to be here, so what would have happened then?' But there's always something to do; there's always something to fill the time with.

Still, life is not about working yourself into the ground. So when I do need time off, I take it. I would hate to reach a point where I wasn't enjoying what I'm doing because I was just so weary of everything. It's important to be able to put all my effort and energy into my work, my music, videos and shoots. It has to be a hundred per cent of me. It can't be fifty per cent. So every now and then I need to relax and take a break.

Travelling can sometimes affect the voice. Tonsillitis and throat infections are terrible for a singer, because you can't do anything while you've got them. You just have to rest until they go, which is really annoying.

I once heard Andrea Bocelli say that your voice is an instrument. You can't just change the strings on it or get a new one, like you can with a guitar; you have to look after your voice properly, because it's the only one you've got. Vocal strain is important to watch for. Some singers have to take a lot of time out to recuperate after over-straining their voice. I really want to avoid that possibility. I don't just want to hammer out the songs now; I want to carry on singing for the rest of my life. It would be awful to be told that I couldn't sing, or to find that my voice had gone, ten years down the line.

People can say, 'OK, you're doing a show here, singing there, doing this and that, here and there.' But I'm the only one that knows how I feel and how my voice feels, so I'm the only one who can decide if my voice isn't going to be able to hold up through all of that. I know if something is going to be too much strain, or if there's too much going on. There's quite a lot of pressure on me to do as much as possible, but I have to strike a balance and protect my voice, so that I'm not out for long periods of time with flu or throat problems.

I just make sure I look after myself. Thankfully, I've got a really understanding team around me who listen when I say I need a break. I push myself, of course; I try to do as much as I can. I want to take all of these fantastic opportunities and make the most of them. However, missing one thing is better than missing ten things because you have to take time out, so I'd rather be cautious than overdo it.

I hadn't slept for three days when I got back from South Africa. The next day was free, so I thought, 'Maybe I should just spend the whole day sleeping.' That seemed the sensible option.

But instead of staying in bed, I got up and went to the riding stables near where I live. Despite my tiredness, I had a really strong urge to go and see the horse that I often ride there. It was the right decision, as it turned out. It set me up for the whole week. It's amazing how riding takes my mind off everything and helps me to chill out and relax.

I love horses. They are amazing animals. Just being around them makes me happy; I don't have to go to the stables and ride. I'm content watching them in the fields or grooming them.

My mum's always loved horses too and we used to ride in Wales for fun. When I was ten, I started wanting to ride every weekend, so I found some stables down the road and my dad took me there every Saturday. Later on, I volunteered to muck out every weekend.

Like a lot of girls, I was horse-mad as a kid. I had books about different breeds and manuals on how to look after a horse. I really wanted my own horse and I tried to convince my mum to get me one, but of course it didn't happen. It was expensive enough to go riding every single week. Then, when I got to thirteen, I wanted to do my music as well – not forgetting ballet, which was another great love of mine! It was quite a lot of expense for my parents to shoulder and I had to make some difficult choices.

So I stopped riding and carried on with ballet until I was sixteen, along with tap and jazz as well. At one point, I wanted to be a ballet dancer, but it wasn't realistic. It involved so much dedication and I was more into my music, really; then music took over.

But of course I went back to riding. I loved it too much not to. Lately I've been doing a lot of school-based riding. Sometimes I go hacking through the fields, but I also love riding around an arena. I'm focusing more on dressage and jumping these days and I find it very peaceful to be in an arena with just the horse and an instructor. It is very challenging learning how to stretch the horse and how to exercise your own muscles for dressage events.

To ride well, you have to be completely in tune with the horse and with yourself, so that you're really connecting. I don't know of any other activity that gives you a similar experience. I find it takes me to a place where I can feel free, let go of everything and just chill out for an hour or two.

When I was young, I didn't think about whether the horse liked me to get on its back and tell it to walk or run or trot, but I began to question these things as I grew older. I stopped riding for a while because I wasn't sure if it was right for the horses. 'Do they like to be ridden?' I wondered. But now I genuinely think that they do, especially when you have a relationship with them. Also, most of the time they are stabled, so they love the exercise.

I certainly don't believe in making an animal do something it doesn't want to. I always listen to what the horse wants to do. But it's a two-way thing when you've got a good relationship, and it feels like you're helping each other.

I was riding around the arena once and there was a jump right in the middle. Now, I didn't tell the horse to jump, because I didn't know much about its past: whether it was a jumper or an all rounder. Nevertheless, when the horse saw the jump, it went towards it and jumped over it. I can only assume that it jumped because it wanted to!

They look after the horses very well at the stables I go to. It's not a fancy stables, but the horses are loved and looked after, and you can see that they're happy. That's what it's about really. I'd never want to ride an unhappy horse.

I'd love to have a horse of my own, one day. I've been on the brink of buying one so many times. I feel a bond with the horse that I ride in England and I'm always showing it loads of love, but it would be different if I bought one. I would really want to be able to own a horse properly and build a strong relationship with it.

I have a Rottweiler named Rome, who stays in the country with friends, as I travel so much. He has dogs and other animals around him, so he really enjoys himself.

Horses are harder to read than dogs, which is why I find them so intriguing. They don't have a tail that wags or tucks between the legs. I guess you can tell something from their ears, because if they're forward, they're being attentive to you, but it's nothing like as clear cut as it is with dogs. So you have to be much more in tune with what they're feeling. When you do have a bond with a horse and you can feel that they're bonded with you, it's really special.

Earlier this year, I leased a beautiful horse in Los Angeles. She's called Sabrina and she's really tall and sunkissed, with a blonde mane. When Mum saw her, she said, 'Hey, you've found your sister!' Funny. I love taking her out.

Topanga Canyon is one of my favourite places in LA; canyon riding is just amazing and the landscape is breathtakingly beautiful. It's the kind of place that you can totally let go, be at one with nature and feel free. That's my idea of heaven.

Outside of music, animals are my main passion. I feel an infinite connection with animals. I don't know: maybe I was an animal in a past life, because I connect with them more than I do with people sometimes! I can't bear to see an animal in distress or in pain. I literally cannot watch those RSPCA adverts where you see dogs being mistreated, because any abuse of animals makes me feel physically sick. It's just horrible and I'll cry. So I'm very passionate about standing up against animal abuse and getting my views across.

When I was twelve, I became a vegetarian for ethical reasons. It was then that I started to become more conscious of where meat comes from and I found that I just didn't want to put it into my body anymore. I love animals, so why would I eat them? Some people love animals and eat them, but I guess I love them more…

My parents were very supportive. They simply said, 'Vegetarian pasta then?' They're not big meat eaters, they mainly eat fish, so it was fine with them. I don't eat fish, though. I'm quite a fussy eater. I love beans on toast. I love tofu and brown rice. I love stir-fry tofu, Pad Thai and spaghetti with Quorn mince. I'm also a cheese-oholic. I try and eat as many vegetables as possible, but I hate cooking them. It takes up so much time!

I turned down the offer to open the Harrods sale at the end of 2008, because Harrods sells fur and I don't believe in killing animals for fur. Even if you do eat meat, I don't believe you should be wearing fur, because it's not a by-product of what you are eating. Hunters slaughter animals specifically for their fur. It's just so evil; it's disgusting and horrible. So I could never justify being paid to promote the sale of fur, even indirectly. It wasn't a million pounds that I was offered, as the papers reported, but even if it had been, I still would have turned it down. I can't go against my principles; I wouldn't be able to sleep at night.

Refusing that money didn't matter to me, because I believe in karma and I think I'll gain rich rewards somewhere else from doing the right thing. At the end of the day, who knows if we're going to be here tomorrow? You can't take anything with you, so it's important to enjoy life and live by your morals. Never go against what you believe in.

Whatever you do, especially if you're in the public eye, there's always going to be some negativity and some positivity surrounding it. The majority response to turning down Harrods was very positive. People said, 'Well done! That's great.' Then there was the negative side: 'How can she turn down that money when she could have given it all to an animal charity?' To me, it would not make any sense to take the money and give it to charity, because that would have been condoning fur at the same time as helping to combat it. It definitely made more sense to make a statement and take a stand.

A few years before the issue of Harrods came up, I started thinking, 'If I don't want to eat animals, why would I wear them?' These days, I just can't bring myself to do it. Wearing leather is not as bad as wearing fur, but it's along the same lines, because it's still an animal that you're wearing as a fashion accessory.

I'm passionate about people having a choice when it comes to leather. If you don't want to wear leather but you want a really nice pair of boots or a bag, you should be able to have nice non-leather boots and a nice non-leather bag. Equally, you should be able to go to good restaurants and find great vegetarian food on every menu, not simply two 'vegetarian options'. I don't like couscous, I don't like aubergines and I don't like mushrooms! Which means that often I can't eat anything!

It's great to be able to speak out about these things and be heard. One of my heroes is Princess Diana, who did so much work for what she believed in. My mum always talked about her when I was young and I admire what she did so much. I know she was a princess and in some ways it was easier for her to get involved, but she didn't have to, not to the extent that she did. She genuinely seemed to empathise with disadvantaged and suffering people.

When it comes to animal rights and compassion, you've got people like Stella McCartney and her sister Mary working towards a higher consciousness. The ideas are slowly catching on and there are vegan lines of bags and clothes appearing. I think it's great, but they need to be more widely available.

I would love to help produce a line of shoes and bags made out of synthetic materials, using no animal products. I would want them to be affordable, cool and fashionable, because some of the vegan shoes and bags out there aren't particularly attractive. In fact, a lot of the cheaper stuff that you find is pretty rubbish; as a result, people think it's very unfashionable to be vegan or vegetarian. But one day I'm hoping to make a really gorgeous, affordable, animal-friendly line of products and aim them at the Topshop market. So we'll see.

Everyone loves to get dressed up to go out somewhere special – and I'm no different. I'm very lucky to have access to some very beautiful clothes; I've come a long way from glueing diamante onto my show dresses! Generally, my red carpet outfit is properly tailored and fitted, whereas my performance outfit needs to be a little bit freer. I like wearing boned corsets, but you have to be able to breathe when you're singing. In fact, you have to be totally happy with what you're wearing when you're singing, so it's important to be practical about what you choose.

I've always loved pink clothes and feminine dresses: when I was younger I loved to prance around the house wearing a tutu. But I've also got a very tomboyish side and I love my boots and my jeans. I've got both aspects: tomboyish from my brothers and feminine from my mum, I guess. It's funny how your fashion sense changes, though. My biggest fashion mistake was buying huge Spice Girls wedges. They were awful, but I loved them at the time. Still, some things never change. Going to Topshop was always a really big treat and I still love going now.

2008 ended with a return trip to *The X Factor* studios, where I performed 'Run'. It was great to be back there, where it all started for me, and I left the studios brimming with happy memories. A few days afterwards, I celebrated a quiet family Christmas at home, doing all the traditional things, before packing up and heading off to Los Angeles in the New Year to start work on my new album.

DREAM BIG

I felt quite a lot of pressure when it came to making the new record. The same old thoughts began to surface: will I be able to find great songs? Will people like what I do? Thankfully, I was able to do quite a bit of riding, which always helps me to escape the stresses of work and forget my worries. Simon Cowell was as supportive as ever. 'Your album won't be coming out until we've got a great, great album, just like I said to you the first time,' he told me. So that was a comfort.

I rented my own apartment by the sea in Santa Monica, which was exciting. I've never actually lived on my own, so I felt very independent. It was all fine until one night a couple of weeks after I moved in: I was fast asleep when I heard a strange noise. I thought it was a helicopter outside, at first, but when I opened my eyes, I looked up to see a huge flying spider the size of my hand, hovering above my head.

As you've probably gathered by now, I hate anything with multiple legs that flies! First I screamed and jumped out of bed; then, feeling very alone, I started crying. I tried to call the night porter, but no one was answering the phone. Meanwhile, this huge thing kept flying around, buzzing near my head.

There was nothing for it but to call up Lou in England. It was about three o'clock in the morning in LA, which is eleven in the morning in London.

'Lou, what shall I do?' I sobbed.

'Don't worry, you'll be fine,' he kept saying.

I tried my best to get the bug out of the apartment, but it was like a crazy thing and kept zooming towards me, as if to attack me. Just then, I remembered that there was a spare room in the apartment. In my panic, and partly because I was still half asleep, my mind had shut down and I had totally forgotten about it! So I slammed the door to my bedroom to shut in the bug and slept in the other room. Sadly, by the next day it had died, which is probably why it was going crazy all night. I was told that all these massive insects come in over the water and you have to put up with them if you live by the sea.

Later, Lou laughed at my reaction. 'You're so stupid!' he said. So I had to remind him that when we had mice in our house in London, he screamed like a girl when he saw one. Now, I'm not scared of mice. I think they're cute, although I get a bit jumpy if they're running around the flat. It's just spiders that freak me out.

The next couple of weeks passed without any more drama, but then my electricity was cut off. My management was dealing with the household bills and they got confused and didn't pay the electricity bill. So I lived by candlelight for a couple of days, which was quite funny. It was also a bit annoying, because the food in the fridge went off! Still, it fascinated me to think about how people managed in the days before electricity. It really fired my imagination to imagine those big scary Victorian houses lit by gas or candles. What a nightmare! I suppose that's why everyone got up at the crack of sparrows in those days.

Soon I started turning into an early riser, but for different reasons. My apartment had no curtains, only white blinds, so my bedroom was flooded with light as soon as the sun came up. As a result, I found it difficult to sleep past seven in the morning, even when I wanted to have a lie in.

I found that I quite like going to bed early and getting up early. In fact, I actually prefer it. Los Angeles is very geared towards daytime, anyway, and the lifestyle is very outdoorsy. Plus, my apartment was right by the beach, where everyone jogs in the early morning.

In the end, I moved out of the apartment. But I stayed in Santa Monica, because even though it gets the crazy flying bugs, in the valley they get tarantulas, apparently. And I'd rather have the crazy flying things than the big tarantulas!

Making the album has been great so far. The whole experience feels different to making the first album. Back then I was in a hotel and flying back and forth to different places, but now I've been mainly based in LA, a bit more settled in my own apartment. It was quite lonely last time, but this time my family has been able to come stay with me, so it's been a much happier experience. I've also been able to work with all the people that I really, really want to work with, because people know me now and what I'm about.

It's great to be able to work with some of the people who worked on my last album, like Ryan Tedder and Claude Kelly, because I've already built up relationships with them. When you work with someone new, it can be difficult, because you need at least a day to get to know each other's likes and dislikes, and then a few more days to really get into your stride. But people you know already have a feel for what you like and where you're heading, so it's easier. They know the way you work and you know the way they work.

I enjoy working with Ryan so much. He is such a cool guy and I really get along with him. I just think he's so talented and musically we totally get each other. We really connect. He puts his all into everything he does and he brings that out in me, so he's very inspiring to work with. He's got so much energy.

Still, it's good to have the spark of the new and meet different people. Sometimes it doesn't work out: you're not really feeling it and it's not going the way you envisioned it would go. But sometimes it's like magic.

I was thrilled to get into the studio with Justin Timberlake, who is a very nice person. Obviously I was nervous when I first met him, because everyone loved 'N Sync when I was younger and Justin Timberlake was a huge pin-up. But it's different when you meet someone. People are just people, after all.

I felt that it was key to find people who I was inspired by. I've had a brilliant time working with John Shanks, who has worked with Natasha Bedingfield, Bon Jovi, Sheryl Crow and did a lot of the last Take That album. He's a hugely talented guy who works from his own studio at Henson Recording Studios in LA and we clicked from the moment we met. He's been a real inspiration.

I was at John's studio one day with my A&R guy, Tim, listening to music. Tim popped out to use the restroom and when he got back he looked a little pale. 'What is it?' I asked him.

'While I was in the bathroom, I felt someone tap me very hard on the shoulder,' he said. 'I turned around but there was nobody there.'

When he came out, the studio manager was walking by. 'Have you seen anyone walk out of the restroom?' he asked her.

'No. No one has come by for a while,' she said.

When Tim told her what had just happened, she said that what he described was quite a common occurrence at Henson. Apparently, people hear and see unusual things in the studio there. 'Perhaps it is connected with the fact that so many of the old rock stars that used to record there have now passed on?' she suggested. I listened avidly to Tim's story, because I am quite a believer in being able to feel energies and presence.

Later that night, I was recording in John's booth. It's quite a large space and has a really eclectic vibe in there. It's filled up with old vinyls, lots of amplifiers, guitars and keyboards, and a massive portrait on canvas of John Lennon playing his guitar. There was also a beautiful old grand piano in the booth, which I thought was really cool. On a little break from singing, I was sipping my lemon tea and surveying the studio when all of a sudden I heard loud music coming from the piano. I looked over at it and froze, unable to believe my eyes! The piano keys were slamming away, playing a song.

My heart pounding, rendered utterly speechless, I dropped my tea. A chill passed through my entire body and I started to shake. 'John!' I screamed.

Just as John came dashing into the room, the piano abruptly stopped playing. 'John! The piano!' I said, struggling to get the words out.

'What's wrong?' he asked urgently.

'The piano started playing by itself,' I stuttered.

He went over to inspect it. Reaching underneath it to a box that was attached to the underside, he said, 'You silly girl! You must have knocked the auto play.' He pushed a button and the piano began playing a tune! We burst out laughing. Then I went into the engineering room to calm down for a while. Although I probably did knock the box, there's still a part of me that thinks maybe it was one of the old rockers slamming down those keys: maybe it was John Lennon himself. I never did find the riff I heard playing on the piano programmed into the box...

I loved working with John. I've also really enjoyed working with a writer called Savan Kotecha, who is part of Max Martin's camp of writers. He has been a real driving force during the making of this album and, with his help, I've found my voice and lyrics.

Of course, everyone expects me to be working with all the big producers, which I am and I love, but I also wanted to try new people and new talent. 'I'm so happy working with all these big names,' I told David Gray, the A&R guy on this album, 'but I also want fresh people involved. I want to work with somebody new and up and coming, like I did last time, with Ryan Tedder.' He took that on board, and came down to the studio one day and said to me 'I've got a great idea for you to work with this amazing young guy called Julian Bunetta. I think you two would be an incredible match in the studio.'

'OK,' I said. If you really believe in him, I'll give it a go.'

So Nicola and I went to visit Julian at his home studio, which he has built in an outhouse on his family's ranch in Malibu Canyon. I loved it even before we pulled up, because there were horses in the fields and dogs running around everywhere. It was a complete oasis!

I instantly felt at home. This is where I'll find the soul of the album, I thought excitedly. On my breaks, I could go and see the horses or play with the dogs, which was just amazing for me. And in Julian I've found a great collaborator: there's a real musical connection and he's also a good friend.

Early in the year, I released another single, 'I Will Be' and shot a really interesting video to go with it, with Melina, the director of the original 'Bleeding Love' video. We wanted to create a film-like quality to the video and were originally hoping to capture it in one continuous shot. Up until then, most of my videos had been composed of lots of quick, edited shots and I was keen to do something different. Sometimes I feel as if long shots can be more emotive than one- and two-second shots, especially when you're singing. The first time I experimented with this idea was on the 'Run' video, where the camera followed me as I was walking through the forest. The result really inspired me and I wanted the same kind of thing for 'I Will Be', something very fluid.

I used Melina because she's really passionate and committed. She knows me, she knows what I like, and her lighting is really pretty. She absolutely knows what she's doing, so I knew she could pull it off, if anyone could. Unfortunately, we only had one day to shoot the whole video, so we didn't manage the one continuous shot. Still, the shots were really long and not a whole lot of editing was required, so I was really pleased with the result.

In January, I was totally over the moon to be nominated for three Grammy Awards. The Grammys are America's biggest music awards, so they're a really big deal. A few days afterwards, I had a meeting with Clive Davis to discuss material for my album. I was really hoping that Clive would ask me to sing at his pre-Grammy party, because Clive's party for the Grammys is *the* party to go to and it means a lot to perform there.

In the months leading up to it, I kept telling people, 'I really want to sing at Clive's party!' I had performed 'Bleeding Love' the year before, but had been so nervous that I didn't really get to enjoy it as much as I wanted to. 'This time,' I thought, 'I can enjoy it more because I'll feel much more at ease.' But first he had to ask me.

When the subject of the Grammy party finally came up, Clive and I had been chatting about material for the album for quite a while. 'Please ask me to sing; please ask me to sing!' I was thinking.

'So, Leona,' he said. 'This year, I want you to come back and I want you to sing.'
'Yes!' I thought. 'He asked!'

So many events go on around the Grammys, including lots of different parties. Two nights before Clive's party, I went to the Timbaland and Rihanna party for a little while, which was really fun. I spent the next day relaxing with my family and then Clive's pre-Grammy party was the following day.

I spent all day getting ready at the Beverley Hilton hotel in Beverley Hills, where the party was being held. I had a real nightmare with the dress I wanted to wear. Everything was fine at first, but suddenly we had to give it back, because the designer wanted whoever wore it to wear it on the red carpet at the Grammys, not at the pre-Grammy parties.

I tried on loads of other dresses, but nothing looked as good. All of a sudden, the runners were knocking on the door telling us that it was time to go to the party. I tried on yet another dress, but it just didn't feel right. So Jen the stylist's assistant, Holland, made one last phone call to the designer. 'I've got Leona here. Your dress looks amazing on her. Are you sure you don't want her to wear it?'

'OK, if she wants to wear it that badly, she can!' the designer said.

Nicola, Jen, Holland and I all screamed and did a little dance around the room. I put the dress on in thirty seconds flat and ran out the door. It all happened in a crazy last minute rush.

When I arrived I found that I was really nervous again. Why? Well, Prince was on the table in front of me, for starters, and Whitney Houston was sitting on the table next to me. It was impossible not to be star struck. At long last I met Jennifer Hudson. She is awesome and I had wanted to meet her ever since I heard her sound check at Clive's pre-Grammy party in 2007. I think she's so inspirational. She has achieved so much and I really admire her. I didn't say any of that, though. I just said that I love what she does, I think she's amazing, she's got an amazing voice and I'm a big fan of what she does! Jennifer told me that she really likes my music and she listens to my album. It's so strange to imagine her driving around listening to my songs or sitting at home playing my album. I felt quite honoured, because she is so talented.

I also met Kelly Clarkson: she was really cool. 'Hey, you sang my song, 'A Moment Like This!' she said. It was weird to think that she had sung it originally when she won American Idol.

P Diddy came up to me and said, 'I really like what you're doing. We should do some work together.'

'OK, cool, let's do it!' I said. I saw him at the Grammys as well and he came up for another little chat. It's amazing to think he actually knows who I am.

After a while, I got a bit over-excited. So before I went on stage, I went upstairs to my room, lay down for a while and chilled out, so that I could be in the right frame of mind when I went on. When I came down, I got up on stage and sang 'Bleeding Love'. Ryan Tedder accompanied me on the piano, which was really cool.

Jennifer Hudson sang as well. She was amazing. Last on was Whitney Houston, who sang a medley that included, 'I'm Every Woman' and 'I Will Always Love You'. It was so great to see her up there. She was really good and she looked wonderful. My mum was crying during her performance and calling out, 'Go Whitney!'

'Mum, that's so embarrassing!' I chided.

It was a really great night, but the rumours connecting me with what happened between Rihanna and Chris Brown afterwards were crazy. Obviously I know Rihanna. I see her out and about and we always have a little catch-up about our music and videos. I think she's so great and so talented; she's got real vision and I love how innovative she is, so I really respect her. But I don't really know Chris at all. I've only ever met him really briefly.

It's terrible that people can make up anything they want and put it out there. No one knows what actually happened that night, so the rumour connecting me with it is the most ridiculous thing I've ever heard in my life. Someone must have rubbed their hands together and thought to themselves, 'Let's see what we can invent. Who was at the party? How about Leona Lewis?'

It upset me that my record company was forced to issue a statement. Usually you just let those things lie until they go away. But people were phoning up so much that I was forced to say that I was at the party with Lou and my family and had 'nothing whatsoever to do with any argument that may have ensued between Chris and Rihanna.' I wish it hadn't been necessary.

I didn't win anything the next day at the Grammys, but all the British artists did really well, from Estelle, Duffy and Adele to Coldplay, so I was really pleased about that. I was very happy for myself, too: being nominated for three Grammys was just insane and I was thrilled to think that people on the Grammy committee had actually been thinking about me. It was a fantastic night and it was just amazing to be a part of it. I felt really proud; I'm going to work hard towards being a part of it again in the future.

The day after the Grammys, I went bowling with my brother Bradley and my nephew Brandon, which was hilarious. The whole family dotes on Brandon. He's nine and so, so, so sweet, so cute, so intelligent and smart and forward for his age. Can you tell that I absolutely adore him?

People ask me if I'm struck by the contrast between glamorous nights out and doing ordinary things – and yes I am, kind of. It's incredible that I can be sitting in my house in my pyjamas, surfing on my computer, thinking back to the week before when I was at a Grammy party sitting opposite Prince.

Sometimes it hits me and I think, 'I can't believe it!' But people like Prince probably sit around in their pyjamas as well. They're great at what they do and that's what I admire them for, but they go bowling and do normal stuff, as well – I think! Personally, I don't really know them, but I'm sure they're just normal people.

My life has changed a lot since *The X Factor*, but I'm still the same person. On my birthday this year I went round the corner from my house in Hackney to a nice little Thai restaurant, with all my girlfriends and my little goddaughter, who is four.

I still have little parties at my house: just me, my friends and family enjoying good music and dancing and food. Everyone has to get up and dance; every single boy in my family thinks he's a DJ, so we've got plenty of DJs and good music on hand.

I always remember who I am and where I come from. I'm the same me now that I always was: I was shocked when my first single got to No. 1; I was shocked when my first album got to No.1; I was shocked when the repackage of the album got to No.1; and I was speechless when I heard about the record-breaking sales of 'Run'. I was so shocked at all of these things!

It's almost like I can't fathom it, but I'm just so glad that the music is reaching so far. That's what's important to me: doing what I do and connecting with people.

I've been really lucky in so many ways. Compared with other people I've seen in the papers, who literally get hounded, I've had it quite easy with the press, perhaps partly because I avoid certain places and know where to go. I've only been bothered by the paparazzi a couple of times. When I went on holiday to Antigua with Lou, I didn't realise we were being followed. But then my mum rang and said, 'There are pictures of you on the internet!'

I was like, 'Oh my God!' It was just really embarrassing. No one wants their bikini pictures splashed all over the papers. I wouldn't even take them myself! But you know, it happens. You just have to accept it and be more wary next time. At least I know how to avoid it when I'm at home.

I'm very excited about the future. Now I've recorded most of my second album, I'm looking ahead to touring next year. I'm just starting to plan my tour and where I'll be playing, so it's all in the early stages. I haven't got into the creative discussions yet, but I'm super-excited about it. It will touch my heart to be given the chance to meet and experience my fans all over the world. It's so important to me for people to see me live on stage. It's where I feel most at home and it's my thank you to everyone for their continued support and love: my fans make all of this possible.

Touring will be a challenge – a real challenge – but I think I'm ready for that next step now. It will definitely round me out as an artist and accelerate me musically. For the next few months, I'll be focusing on my voice and my performing skills, along with my piano and guitar playing. I want to keep on improving all the time, so I just can't wait.

Looking back on the last few years, I feel there's a lot to be proud of. I'm especially grateful to my family and friends for staying close throughout the journey. I certainly couldn't have made it without them, or without all the people who have supported me and bought and downloaded my music. So much has happened and I feel sure that there's so much more to come. I've fulfilled many of my ambitions – and done things I didn't even imagine were possible, including performing in front of billions of people in Beijing! I think that probably has to be my proudest moment so far, but I'm not finished yet. There's so much more that I want to do.

My ambitions and aspirations for the future are huge. Music will always come first for me: I have so much more to share and give. I've also discovered on this amazing journey how much I love taking a creative role in all the different aspects of my career: I'm going to continue to learn and grow when it comes to my photo shoots, performances and more. I'm a huge movie fan and would love to try acting at some point. It's something I touched on in the 'I Will Be' video with Chace Crawford and the experience made me hungry to delve further.

I also want to start a clothing and accessory range that's completely ethical, giving people the chance to shop with choice. And I will be working on developing my charity work and trying to make a big difference where I can: there are so many great causes that need my help.

I feel very thankful for all the wonderful, amazing opportunities I have been given. I'm so lucky to be able to travel and perform and enjoy so many experiences through my music. I have always wanted to sing and perform, and it's amazing to think that I am actually doing what I dreamed of doing. I hope that, through this book, this little window into my life, I can show that everything is achievable. Don't ever limit yourself: dream big.

Previous pages:
Horsing around with friends in L.A.

Following pages:
Getting ready for Clive Davis' party, Beverley Hills, February 2009

Following pages:
Zurich Arena
Madison Square Gardens, NYC, with Rhianna and Natasha Bedingfield

With Mum and Dad

I Will Be video shoot, NYC, December 2008

With Jennifer Hudson

Recording for the new album, Hollywood, 2009

David Letterman day, NYC

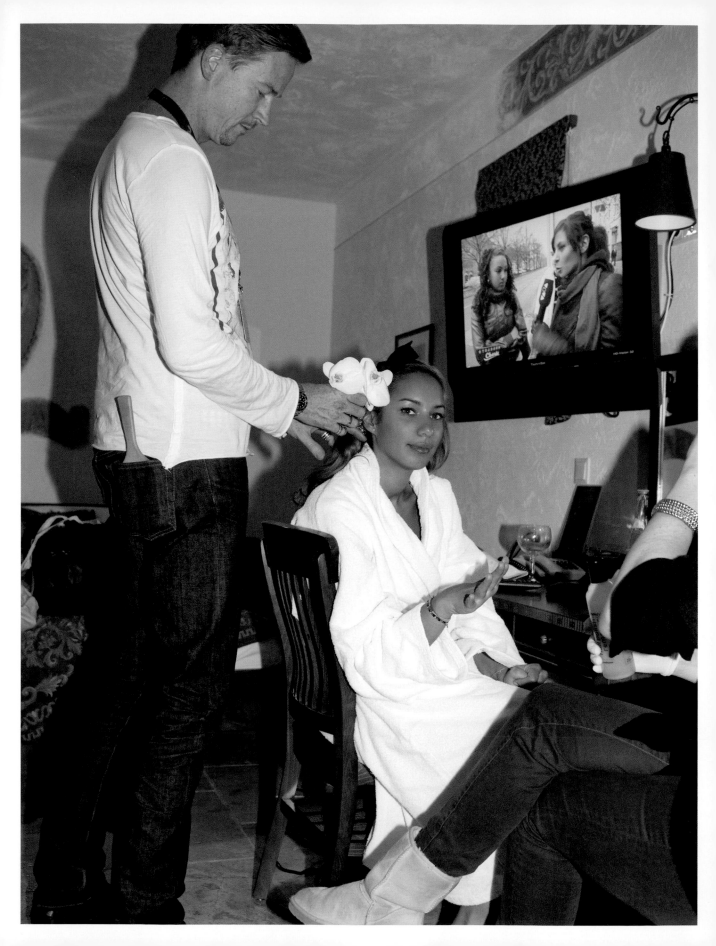

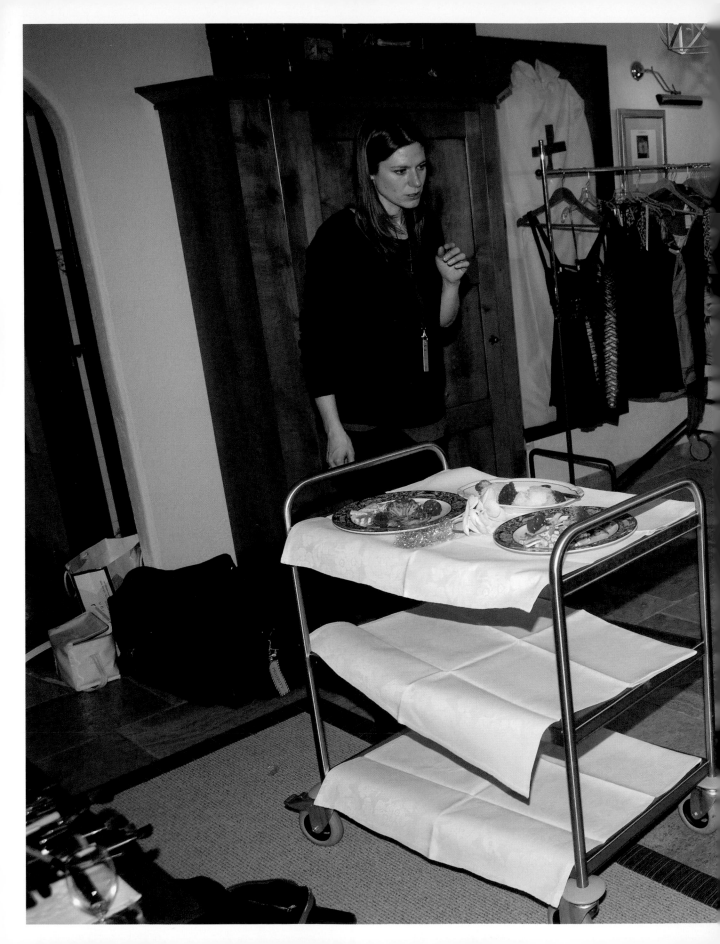

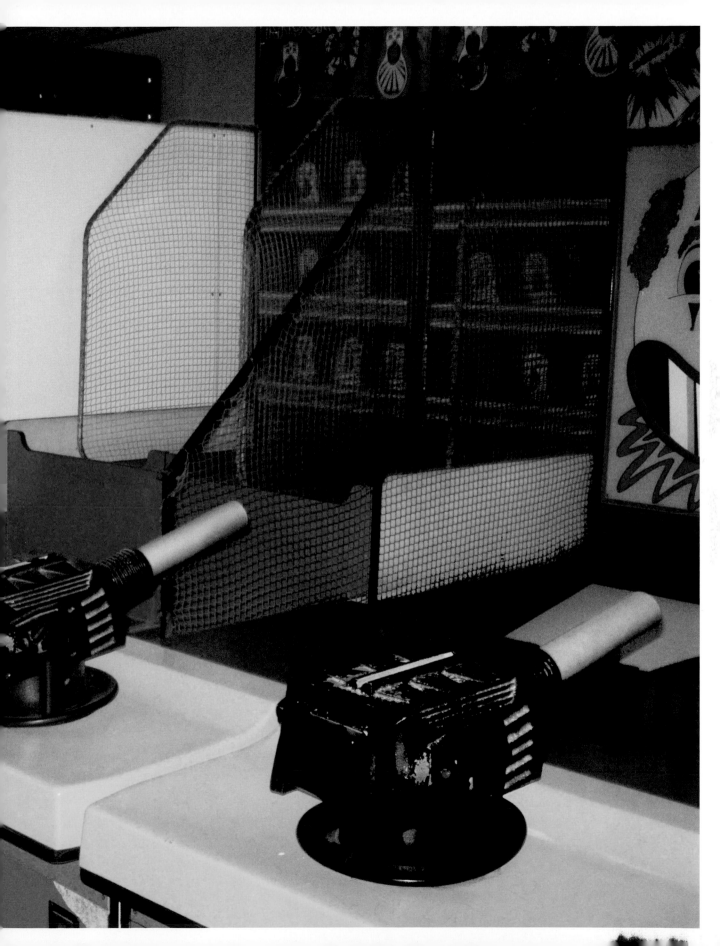

Previous pages:
Justin Timberlake's party
Time off and peforming in NYC

Following pages:
Morning of the Grammys, with my nephew, L.A.
In the afternoon, ready for the Grammys
Bowling in Santa Monica
Las Vegas
Opening of *Westfield* Centre, London

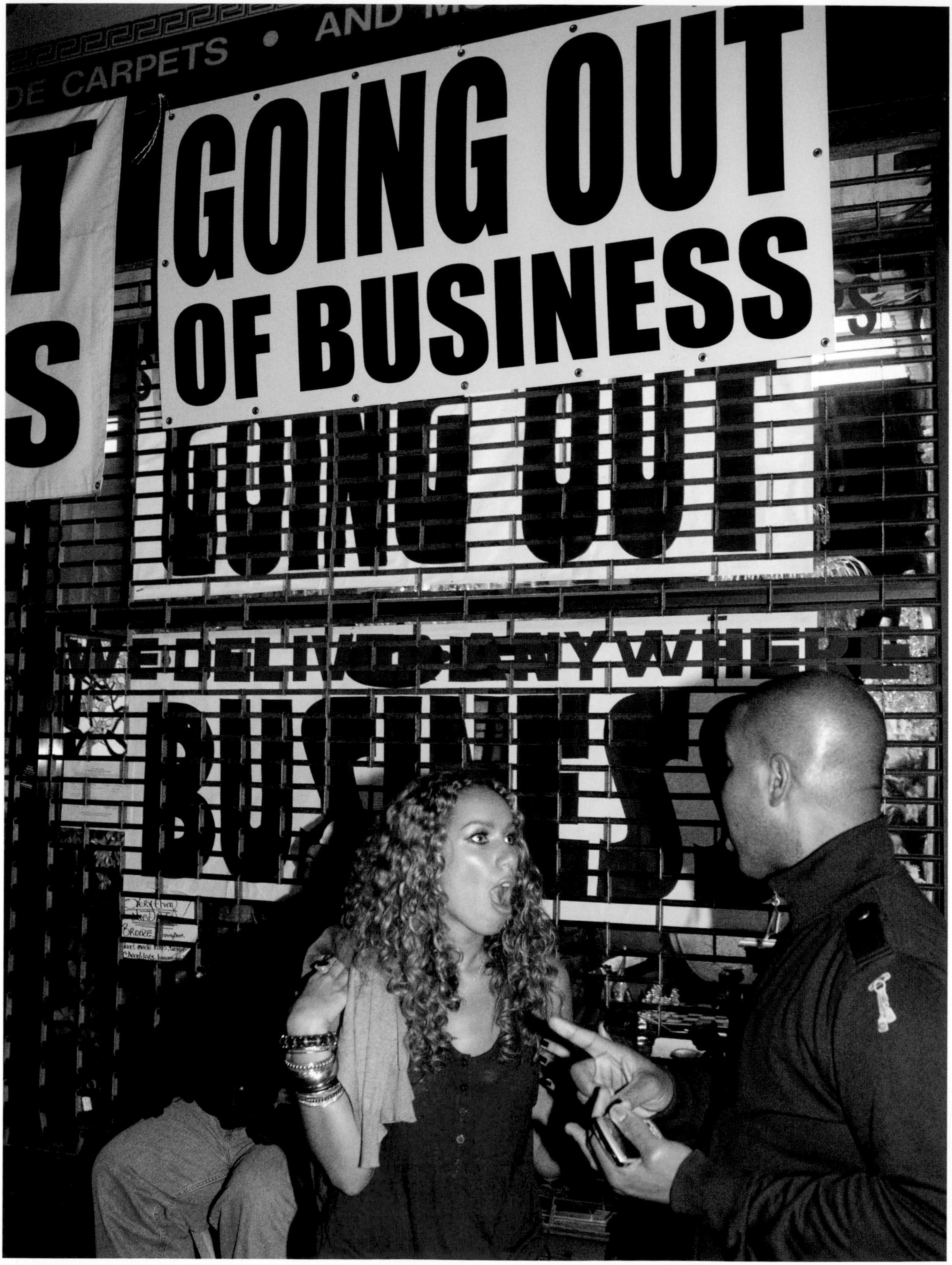
GOING OUT
OF BUSINESS

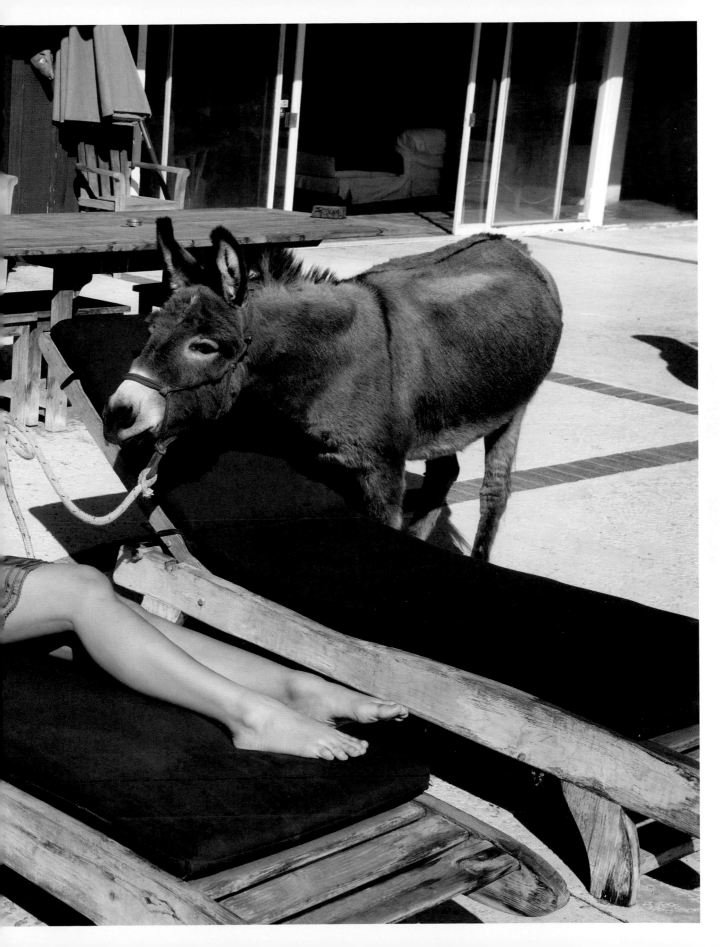

Backstage at GMTV and ITV Divas

Following pages:
ITV Divas
X Factor rehearsal with choreographer Priscilla, and performance

From previous page:
In L.A.

Following pages:
In L.A.
With my Dad, Joe
At GMTV
Leaving home in Santa Monica for the Grammys

LEONA LEWIS

Firstly I thank God for being with me each day, for the blessings I receive and for all that is good in this world.

Thank you mum and dad for always being there, encouraging, nurturing and believing in me.

Thank you to my brothers Bradley and Kyle, for always supporting me.

Thank you to my best girlies Aysha and Yasemin for always being there for me.

Thank you Lou for all your love and for always standing beside me.

Thank you my wonderful Aunty Laurette, Dean and Dyonne, for all the love you show.

Thank you my lovely Aunty Sue, Uncle Ron, Uncle Terry, Aunty Lined, Lee and Jade for all of your support.

Thank you all of my beautiful friends and family, for all of your caring kindness and belief.

Thank you Nicola for always being there on every step of this new journey.

Thank you Richard, Harry and everyone at Modest that's helped along this journey.

Thank you Steve Martin for your constant hard work, support and honesty; I found a friend in you.

Thank you Hodder for your vision and support throughout the creation of my book.

Thank you Ben and Jane — aka glam ma and glam pa — for your dedication and effort.

Thank you Alison, Naomi and Jen for your all of your hard work and creativeness with my styling.

Thank you Dean Freeman for all the passion you have put in to creating such a wonderful piece of work. A picture speaks a thousand words and I will cherish this book as long as I live.

Thank you to everyone taking the time to read and look at my book. To all of my fans worldwide, thank you for your belief and for making all of these oppurtunities possible, I thank you so much for your constant support.

'Shoot for the moon, even if you miss you'll land among the stars'

With love always, Leona-x-

To Leona — Thank you for being my muse and giving me the opportunity to create this wonderful book with you — I respect your pure talent; at times you're a mystery and at the same time deeply alluring with a great sense of humour and modesty. You're an artist and your voice is here to stay, enjoy the journey as it continues and I appreciate having been given the opportunity to share the journey for a brief time. It's been a privilege and a pleasure. You giving me the trust is the reward.

Thank you — Harry Magee and Richard Griffiths, I really appreciate your vision and focus and the opportunity you gave me. Truly great managers, Modest management. To Nicola Carson, what can I say — without you this book would not have happened and your energy and sense of awareness is legendary — a true star of the music and entertainment industry, thank you for putting up with me. Steve Martin — the best tour manager in the business and a gentle and honest man. Stuart Bell — genius P.R, James Sully — master of contracts. Alan Edwards — thanks for the introduction, Terri Manduca (my angel agent), Chris Benson, Joe and Marie Lewis and Lou. Ben Cooke (hair master), Jane (make-up), Naomi (stylist), Jen (stylist) and Kevin Ford (for cover hair). Jamie, Fenella, Lisa, Brett, Ben and all the Hodder team — great publishers. Rebecca Cripps — wonderful work. Joby Ellis — excellent designer, Richard Poulton — digital genius, Toby Dodson (L.A support), David Lyons and Amelia Barrett (L.A home from home), Siobhan Barron, big help at short notice, The Hochulis of Brenwood (your donkey saved my day!), House of Oldies, www.houseofoldies.com, Arnold Hatters, www.arnoldhatters.com, Brendan Paul, www.bestelvis.com, www.gracelandchapel.com, Alexander Goschin © for two horse-riding pictures, pp. 22, 72.

'To my mother Sonny, my inspiration and always sweet in my dreams.'

DEAN FREEMAN
Photographer, publishing consultant, creative director and originator of the original concept for *Leona Lewis — Dreams.*